BIBLE MARRIAGES

by

Patricia L. Welch

Bible Marriages

2013

Welch Publishing ISBN: 978-0-578-13383-6

All Rights Reserved

Printed in the United States of America

Scriptures taken from the Holy Bible, New International Version®, NIV®.
   Copyright © 1973, 1978, 1984 by International Bible Society.
   Used by permission of Zondervan Publishing House
   All rights reserved worldwide
   www.zondervan.com

Scriptures taken from the Scofield Reference Bible, Authorized King James Version
   Copyright © 1967 by Oxford University Press, Inc.
   Used by permission of Oxford University Pess
   All rights reserved worldwide

Table of Contents

Acknowledgements................................4

Introduction......................................5

How to Gain the Most From This Study.............6

Adam and Eve – Perfect Love....................7

Mr. and Mrs. Noah – Faithful, Committed Love....18

Abraham and Sarah – Love With A Promise........29

Isaac and Rebekah – Sweet Love That Soured.....38

Mr. and Mrs. Potiphar – Unfaithful Love........49

Nabal and Abigail – Longsuffering Love.........62

David and Bathsheba – Love With Regrets........73

Mr. and Mrs. Job – A Painful Love..............83

Hosea and Gomer – Unconditional Love...........94

Joseph and Mary – Profound Love...............110

Aquila and Priscilla – Compatible Love........118

Marriage Scrambles..............................129

"For Better or For Worse".......................130

Acknowledgements

Besides thanking God, I want to thank the following people for their invaluable help as I studied, taught, and now publish this book on Bible Marriages.

Professor Chris Miller of Word of Life Bible Institute and Cedarville College, who helped edit my original manuscript and gave me wonderful encouragement. Thank you Chris for your tender heart.

Mrs. Jean Garner who attended my classes, taught my study on Bible Marriages, and wrote a poem to go with each one. Luckily I kept and was able to find the poems and have included them in this book so that they can bless others. Thank you, Jean.

Dr. John W. Reed, author and former professor at Cedarville College and Dallas Theological Seminary who has allowed me to include his first person story of Hosea and Gomer in this book. I first read this story in the 1980's even before it was in print and was so touched by it. Thank you Dr. Reed for your kindness. Check out Dr. Reed's website at www.civilwarstories.org He is currently working with a publisher to republish his out of print books as eBooks and creation of some new works.

The ladies in "Women of Grace" life group who listen to me teach each week and give me valuable feedback and encouragement as I witness spiritual growth in their lives.

And last but not least, a big thank you to my husband, Francis Welch, who faithfully reads over my work, chapter by chapter, makes helpful suggestions, and challenges me to be creative by his insightful questions and comments. ♥

Introduction

Welcome to an insightful journey of Biblical marriages that God has recorded in His Word so that we can learn from them.

When God prompted my heart to write about Bible marriages, I found that one of the most surprising truths revealed by God is that even His people struggle with purity, integrity, character, faithfulness and unconditional love for their marriage partner.

Whether you are single, married, divorced, or considering remarriage, you will be able to gain important knowledge of God's blueprint for marriage. There are valuable lessons to be learned about God and our relationship with others. We live in a society today where marriage has been redefined from God's original purpose to embrace cultural norms that are far outside of God's approval, intent and purpose for marriage. Like Mr. & Mrs. Noah, we need to stand against the tide.

I have had the pleasure of knowing couples who have been married 30, 40, 50 and even 60 years or more. I am thankful to God that my husband and I have been married, over 50 years and our love has grown stronger. It wasn't always that way - it takes commitment, following God's principles, and a big dose of God's grace.

As we study together, you will see not only good Biblical wisdom for marriage, but you will also learn about the character of God and how important it is to know Him if your marriage is to succeed. May God bless you as you study.

Rejoicing in Christ, Pat

How To Gain The Most From This Study

In this generation, busyness and stress abound. Now more than ever, you need to slow down enough to focus on God and His Word. If necessary, plan to start your day earlier in order to get back to the basics of your Christian faith.

Choose a time that is convenient for you and when you are not likely to be interrupted. Find a special place to concentrate on God and what He is going to reveal to you Make Psalm 119:18 the daily prayer of your time with God. "Open my eyes, Lord, that I may see wondrous things in your Law." Stick with it and treat it as an important appointment with God, and keep that appointment no matter what.

Whether you spend 15 minutes or an hour or more each day in the Word of God, ask Him to fill you with His Holy Spirit and to give you wisdom and understanding as you go through this study.

- ♥ Purpose to take the time to read and think about the story carefully, and not rush through trying to answer the questions.

- ♥ Writing out Bible verses is never a waste of time, so take the time to do this. The Word of God is powerful.

- ♥ After you have completed a lesson, take time to read back over both the lesson and your answers, and ask God to impress upon your heart what He wants you to remember and apply to your life. You might want to keep a notebook of these things.

- ♥ Practice "immediate obedience" to anything God tells you to do.

- ♥ Take time to talk to God in prayer after each lesson and thank Him for any insights and wisdom He has given you.

ADAM & EVE
"Perfect Love"

"Every good gift and every perfect gift is from above and comes down from the Father of lights, with whom is no variableness, neither shadow of turning."
James 1:17

Adam and Eve started out with the best chance in history of having a perfect and successful marriage. it's what we all dream about - the perfect couple, the perfect wedding, the perfect setting and perfect circumstances - the ultimate storybook romance.

The Perfect Couple

Where did Adam & Eve come from? Genesis 1:27

_____

They were made in the very image of God; therefore, they were divinely beautiful and perfect.

How did God form Adam? Genesis 2:7

_____

_____

How was Eve formed? Genesis 2:21-22

_____

_____

For what reason did God make Eve for Adam? Genesis 2:18

_____

_____

Being A Good Helpmeet

Accept him unconditionally . . . Philippians 2:3

Stop trying to change him. When you don't feel accepted, you feel insecure, angry and resentful. Acceptance takes the pressure off. God accepts you unconditionally, even with all of your imperfections, and you can do the same for your husband. Your husband may need changing, but you'll be better off leaving that to God.

Admire him. . . Ephesians 2:9

Men crave admiration. Compliment him as much as you can on what he does right, especially in front of others, and try not to criticize because that just tears him down. Build him up and he will be devoted to you.

Adapt to him . . . Philippians 2:4

Accept his schedules and his hobbies and take a genuine interest in what interests him. When he suggests an exciting idea, like taking a course in "conversational Chinese", join in enthusiastically instead of putting a dampener on it. Live on the edge!

Appreciate him . . . Philippians 1:3

Be loyal to him and thankful for him. Have an "attitude of gratitude." Thank him for all the little things you usually take for granted, not only with your words, but with your attitude and actions. Give him your undivided attention.

The Perfect Wedding

God, Himself, brought Eve to Adam (Genesis 2:22). Eve stood there in full womanhood. She was beautiful and complete, an exquisite masterpiece created by God from Adam's rib.

What were Adam's first thoughts about Eve? Genesis 2:23
_____
_____
_____

Then came the marriage ceremony in verse 24:
_____
_____
_____

And then the honeymoon in verse 25:
_____
_____

God showed them His will, they married with His blessing, and began a beautiful, perfect honeymoon, looking forward to spending the rest of their lives together.

The Perfect Setting

They were in the most beautiful place imaginable. It was perfect in beauty because it was brand new, created by God for them.

How is Eden described in Genesis 2:8-9?_____
_____
_____
_____
_____

A further description is found in verse 10a:_____
_____
_____

What does Genesis 2:12 tell us?_____
_____
_____

The Perfect Circumstances

They had no traffic jams, no irritating people, no crime, no sickness, and no pain or tears. They had a perfect relationship with God, had satisfying work to do, and unsurpassed beauty around them.

What did God tell them to do?

Genesis 1:28 _____
_____
_____
_____

Genesis 2:15 _____

Genesis 2:19-20 _____

They were in perfect harmony with themselves, their surroundings, and their God. The last part of Isaiah 51:3 describes what it must have been like:
_____
_____
_____

God placed Adam and Eve in a garden and gave them every good thing they needed in order for them to be joyful and productive. However, there was one thing He withheld from them. What was it and why was it withheld? Genesis 2:16-17
_____
_____
_____

How did the serpent (Satan) challenge God's Word and appeal to Eve's pride? Genesis 3:4-5

_____
_____
_____

Why did Eve disobey God? Genesis 3:6_____

_____
_____
_____

Eve gave some of the fruit to Adam and he ate also. What does I Timothy 2:14 tell us about this situation?

_____

Adam, being the spiritual head of the home, should have been an example to Eve, but instead he also sinned, and all mankind has suffered the consequences.

Write out Romans 5:12:_____

_____
_____
_____

What happened when God confronted them with their sin? Genesis 3:8-13_____

_____
_____

Why should they have admitted it was their own fault and taken responsibility for their sin? James 1:14

_____
_____
_____

The following verses tell us the provision God gives us when the enemy comes to trip us up:

Write out James 4:7 _____
_____
_____

Write out I Corinthians 10:13 _____
_____
_____
_____
_____
_____

Looking upward to God

> ### *** *God is Righteous* ***
>
> He is perfect and holy and requires obedience from His children. He hates sin. We need to go to God, knowing that He hates sin, but also knowing that He will cleanse it from our lives and restore us to fellowship with Him when we openly confess our sin to Him.
>
> Psalm 145:17 _____
> _____
> _____
>
> I John 2:1b _____
> _____
> _____
> _____

From My Heart to Yours . . .

Remember when you were a young girl, perhaps dreaming about your Prince Charming. He was going to be just wonderful and meet your every need, and you would spend each day of your "happily ever after" in perfect joy and bliss.

Now we think to ourselves . . . IF ONLY!

IF ONLY my husband were more loving and romantic
IF ONLY we knew how to communicate better
IF ONLY we had more money and could buy our dream house and afford all the things we desire
IF ONLY my husband would be the Spiritual head of our home
IF ONLY we could spend more time together
And on and on and on.

We think that if everything were perfect, then our marriage would be perfect too. Unfortunately, that is not true as proven by the study we have just completed.

God's original idea of marriage was for two people to live together in harmony and unity of spirit. God created Eve to be a helpmeet for Adam - to be a part of him and encourage him to be all that God wanted him to be. To help him complete the job that God gave him to do and to love him and respect him. So many women are concerned with MY rights, MY plans, MY career, MY pleasure; then they wonder why their marriage does not meet their expectations. God wants you to be a helpmeet for your husband.

If the story of Adam and Eve had ended with all the perfection it started with, we would all go away sighing, "IF ONLY I had those circumstances." "IF ONLY that marriage were mine." But we have no such excuse to relieve our marital responsibilities and attempt to put the blame for our problems elsewhere.

The perfect couple with the perfect marriage, in the perfect setting, with the perfect circumstances, BLEW IT! With one act, they destroyed everything they had and they were no longer perfect. Everything was changed.

Their crime? They disobeyed God, their Creator, and listened to the enemy of their souls. God told them exactly what not to do and what would happen if they disobeyed. This was their God who formed them from the dust of the ground; the One who created the heavens and the earth; the One they had perfect fellowship with in the garden and who always told them the truth.

Yet when Eve was tempted by a different voice, a voice that twisted God's Word and mocked it, she listened and did the thing that God told her not to do. How many times do we do that? We know God loves us and always tells us the truth, yet we disobey Him. We listen to our enemy, Satan, the one who goes about like a roaring lion, seeking whom he may devour, the one who hates God and hates us. And yet sometimes we are tempted to believe his voice instead of God's. How sad, and how perverse is our nature!

The Bible tells us that Eve was deceived but that Adam sinned knowingly (I Timothy 2:14). Adam might have been so afraid of losing Eve that he decided to sin with her and take the consequences. If she died, he wanted to die too. Sometimes we hold on, instead of trusting in God.

Could Adam have done anything differently? Yes! We all choose whether we will obey God or not, and when we stand before God, we will not be able to blame someone or something else for our choices. We are responsible for our own sin.

Adam could have refused the fruit and gone to God on Eve's behalf. Even if God had struck Eve dead on the spot, Adam should have had enough trust in God to know that God would meet his needs in another way. God will not take something we need without replacing it.

Adam chose to cling to Eve and sin with her, and each one of us has felt the consequences of that choice in our lives, for every person since Adam has been born with the sin nature.

Adam and Eve found out that they had no goodness apart from God. That is a lesson that each married couple and each individual must learn.

The Bible describes the human heart in Jeremiah 17:9:
*"The heart is deceitful above all things,
and desperately wicked;
Who can know it?"*

Our deceitful heart is why we have to depend so much on the Word of God. God's Word is not deceitful or wicked - it is absolute truth!

God forgave Adam and Eve and provided for them a covering (Gen. 3:21) so that they need not be ashamed and could continue to meet with God. An innocent animal was slain, and its blood shed to provide the covering. Perhaps this is when God further explained to them (Gen. 3:15) that there would be one who would come and shed His blood so that individuals could be reconciled to God, once and for all.

That One has come!

John 1:29 "...Behold the Lamb of God (Jesus Christ) who takes away the sin of the world."

Jesus said in John 10:27-28 "My sheep know my voice, and I know them, and they follow me. And I give unto them eternal life; and they shall never perish, neither shall any man pluck them out of my hand."

*** Marriage Wisdom ***

1. In order to have the most perfect marriage possible, both partners must put God first and obey Him, trusting Him to supply all their needs.

2. Dedicate your marriage to the Lord and ask Him for wisdom.

3. Stop blaming God, your mate, or circumstances for your imperfect marriage. No marriage is perfect.

4. Give up your unrealistic expectations that your marriage should always be "romantic." It takes sacrificial love (God's love) to make it the best it can be.

5. Purpose in your heart to be committed to your mate and give 100% to your marriage. Do not allow the word "divorce" in your vocabulary.

6. Start practicing "Being A Good Helpmeet" (see page 8).

Adam and Eve went on to live a long life together. They never again had a perfect marriage, but they stayed together and populated the earth as God had told them.

Adam and Eve
by Jean Garner

There never was a marriage that could so fulfill a dream,
He more handsome than a prince, and she his lovely queen!
They were absolutely perfect, fresh right from God's own hand,
There was not a blot or blemish. They were in a perfect land.
She was part of her own loved one, from just beneath his heart.
They would never have a worry, for God their way did chart.
All harmony and unity, and both in perfect health;
No financial worries, the whole world was their wealth!

He loved his bride most dearly, no thought of Women's Lib;
God's exquisite masterpiece, and made from Adam's rib!
It was in a wondrous garden, where they spent their honeymoon;
Trees and streams and birds and flowers, not a trace of gloom.
No traffic jams or crime or pain or sickness or distress;
They could have lived a long, long life of utmost happiness!
If they had heeded God's own Word, in the garden they'd have stayed,
But sad to say, 'twas not the case, for God they disobeyed.

God gave to Eve all lovely things that she could ever need,
But she became dissatisfied; in her heart there entered greed.
Just one thing that God had banned, the stately Tree of Life;
The devil said: "Go eat it; you'll be a smarter wife!"
So she didn't ask her husband; she did not inquire of God,
But ate the fruit and brought a curse upon this sacred sod!
And Adam followed in her wake, so he was guilty too.
She was his wife and in his care, what else was he to do?

And so today young couples hope, as they plan on being wed,
That they'll have a perfect marriage; no worry and no dread!
But since our famous couple brought sin to our fair earth,
Nothing will be perfect, though they try for all they're worth!
If they listen not to Satan, but heed God's Word instead;
Right from the beginning, by the Savior to be led;
It still may not be perfect, and no Eden will be given,
But they can have, while still on earth, a little bit of Heaven!

MR & MRS NOAH
"Faithful Committed Love"

*"When thou passeth through the waters,
I will be with thee . . ."*
Isaiah 43:2

Take time to read Genesis, chapters 6-8, before we begin so you can get an overall look at the story of Noah.

Character of the World in Noah's Day

Genesis 6:5,11-12 gives us a picture of what the world was like in the days of Noah. What is your assessment of the situation?

_____
_____
_____
_____

Because it was such an evil world, what did God decide to do and why? Genesis 6:6-7

_____
_____
_____
_____

Describe the world we live in today and some of the things that go on under the watchful eyes of God:

_____
_____
_____

It makes you wonder how a godly couple like Mr. & Mrs. Noah or how a Christian couple today can live in the midst of such evil.

Character of Noah

Noah had a godly great-grandfather named Enoch. What does Genesis 5:22-24 tell us about him?
_____
_____

Jude 14 and 15 tell us more about Enoch and the message that God gave him for the people of his day. What was Enoch's prophecy?_____
_____
_____
_____

Although Noah never knew his great-grandfather personally, he must have admired him very much as he listened to the stories told about him. And as he heard the message his great-grandfather preached, the fear of the Lord was instilled in his heart.

How can we know that? Write out the following verses and see what conclusion you come to:

Genesis 6:8_____
_____

Genesis 6:9_____
_____
_____

Genesis 7:5_____
_____

How does II Peter 2:5 describe Noah?
_____

How does Hebrews 11:7 describe Noah_____
_____
_____
_____
_____

Noah wasn't a perfect man, but God had mercy on him because Noah feared the Lord. In other words, Noah had an awesome trust in God and a hatred of evil.

Read Psalm 103 and write down statements that prove that if we have the fear of the Lord, God will be merciful to us.

Psalm 103:11_____
_____
_____

Psalm 103:13_____
_____
_____

Psalm 103:17 _____
_____
_____
_____

God spoke personally to Noah and told him about the judgment to come on the earth, and told him to build an ark for the saving of his family. Pretending that you were living back in those days, what might have been some thoughts going through your mind when you saw Noah building this huge boat?_____
_____
_____

Matthew 24:37 holds a warning for this generation. What is it?_____

_____

Matthew 24:38 describes the attitude of the people while Noah was building the ark. What was it?_____

_____

It was business as usual. They weren't concerned about what Noah said was going to happen.

Matthew 24 describes another judgment from God that could occur at any time called The Great Tribulation. It will be a time of horror for the people on earth, and yet there doesn't seem to be much concern about it as people go about doing their business as usual.

Christians are called to be alert and ready, and to warn people about what is to come. Who do you need to tell about Jesus and the coming Judgment of God?

_____

_____

Character of Mrs. Noah

Because the Bible does not record anything bad about Noah's wife, and because she was saved along with Noah and the rest of the family, I think it is safe to assume that Mrs. Noah believed in God.

What does the fact that her children and daughters-in-law were saved suggest to you about Mrs. Noah's character?

_____

_____

When Noah received the judgment message from God and started working on the ark, Mrs. Noah had a lot on her mind also. Put yourself in her sandals and think about what you would plan for a long stay on the ark if God gave such a message today.

Food:_____
_____
_____
_____

Clothes:_____
_____
_____

Medical Supplies:_____
_____
_____

Cleaning Supplies:_____
_____
_____

Cooking Supplies:_____
_____
_____

Things to make the ark seem like home:_____
_____
_____
_____

Things to keep everyone busy on rainy days on the ark:
_____
_____
_____

Things needed later to start a new home:_____
_____
_____
_____
_____

As you can imagine, a great deal of thought had to go into this. Mrs. Noah had to decide what was a necessity and what was a luxury. What things did she really need and what things could she do without. Noah didn't have time to worry about these things, and most likely depended on his wife for wisdom in these areas.

Looking upward to God

**** God is Just ****

God's judgments are perfect, for it is impossible for God to do anything unfair. He keeps His promises and will never go against His Word.

It would be important for Mr. & Mrs. Noah to know this deep within their hearts as they thought of all those outside the ark. God had certainly given those people plenty of warning and opportunity to believe through Noah's preaching.

Psalm 9:8 _____
_____
_____
_____

I John 1:9 _____
_____
_____
_____

From My Heart to Yours . . .

Mr. & Mrs. Noah didn't live in the same world Adam and Eve started out in, a world of beauty and peace. It was a time of great wickedness, violence and rebellion, and in the midst of all the evil around them, they were godly people.

Looking around them at the world in which they lived, they must have sadly reflected on the stories that had been passed down from generation to generation, telling of God's creation and love. Looking at the ugliness that man had made, they must have longed for better days - peaceful days when man could safely raise his family without fear.

They might have envied Adam and Eve in that beautiful garden, and wondered why Eve took the first bite of the forbidden fruit. Now all were born under the curse of sin, sinners just like their parents!

As Noah worked on the ark and thought about the coming judgment, his heart was burdened for his friends and neighbors. He would preach to them about the things of God and warn them about the coming judgment. He told them to turn from their evil ways and to be saved before it was too late.

They must have mocked him and laughed at him, thinking that he was a crazy old man. They went right on with their lives as if nothing was going to happen, and did not listen when God tried to warn them through Noah's preaching.

Noah preached for 120 years without a single convert, and could have gone through times of discouragement and depression, turning to his family for encouragement. Because of that, it would be important that Noah would have an understanding and loving wife.

With all the evil in the world, Mrs. Noah must have been a very positive and godly woman in order to bring up her children to be different from their peers and to fear God. She wasn't out trying to make a name for herself and be noticed. She knew that the most important job she had was to be there for her husband and children.

She not only taught her children, but most likely had to teach her daughter-in-laws about God. Remember, the only people who were saved out of the flood were Noah, his wife, his sons and his daughters-in-law. That means the girls parents did not believe in God, because they weren't saved.

Maybe Mrs. Noah held a Vacation Bible School in her back yard when her sons were little and invited the neighborhood children in to hear Bible stories, sing songs, and learn about God. Three little girls could have come and listened and believed in God.

Or, when her sons got to the age where they wanted wives, and brought their girls home to meet mom, Mrs. Noah might have said, "Wait a minute. First these girls must be trained in the ways of God so they will fit into our family."

Or she could have done such a good job introducing her boys to God that they in turn shared their faith with their girlfriends.

Whatever she did, it made a difference in their lives, and how thankful they must have been for Mrs. Noah.

Mrs. Noah must have been a positive example as she submitted, encouraged, taught and worked hard, but the character quality that impresses me the most is her loyalty and commitment to her marriage partner, which above everything else tells of her faith in God.

How would you feel if the whole world were against your husband? How would you feel about a man that everyone else mocked and thought was crazy? After a while I'd probably begin to wonder if they were right and ask him to tone it down a bit. "After all, you don't have to go around offending people." Rain was unheard of in those days. It had never rained before. Yet her husband was building a large boat so that when the rains came, they would be safe. He was the talk of the town and everyone was gossiping about the crazy old preacher. They probably even had sightseeing tours coming by to view the huge three-story boat and the man who was building it.

If you are the wife of a preacher or teacher of God's Word, a full-time Christian worker, or a Christian who shares the news of the gospel at his job and in the neighborhood, you too have probably faced some persecution. Your husband may face discouragement when no-one seems to understand or care about the message that God has given to him. Consider yourself a privileged person. You have an honor that few women have - to be the helpmeet of a man who is called and set apart by God for a task that will reap eternal rewards. Take a lesson from the wife of Noah and be a loyal wife, committed to your husband and your marriage no matter what. Your husband needs your encouragement and loyalty if he is doing what God has called him to do.

When those first drops of rain started to fall, after God had sealed the door of the ark, the wife of Noah must have fallen to her knees and thanked God for the husband he had given her. All the mocking words and the persecution they went through must have faded away from mind as they lifted their voices in praise to the Lord.

And when the first drops of rain started to fall, the people outside the ark realized that what Noah had been preaching about was true and that God's judgment was upon them. Yet it was too late! God had shut and sealed the door!

Noah and his family must have gone through heartbreak

knowing that now it was too late to help these friends and neighbors Noah had been preaching to for so long. But even in the midst of their heartbreak, Mr. & Mrs. Noah must have clung together, realizing that even with God's judgment all around them, they were safe because of the mercy and grace of God.

An old song comes to mind in thinking about this couple . . .

<u>God Leads Us Along</u>
by G. A. Young, 19th century

In shady green pastures, so rich and so sweet,
God leads His dear children along;
Where the water's cool flow bathes the weary one's feet,
God leads His dear children along.

Some through the waters, some **through the flood**,
Some through the fire, but all through the blood;
Some through great sorrow, but God gives a song,
In the night season and all the day long.
(Emphasis mine)

*** *Marriage Wisdom* ***

No matter what circumstances surround us, God will protect His children if they faithfully live according to His Word. Don't ever be ashamed of the Word of God, even when ridiculed. Cling to God and each other and be faithful.

Mr. & Mrs. Noah had many more years together as husband and wife, and with their family they populated the world once again.

Mr. & Mrs. Noah
by Jean Garner

Since Noah lived upon the earth, five thousand years have passed;
And at that time, the wickedness, almost this age surpassed!
Sin so abounded in his day, the Lord condemned the race;
You'd wonder Noah could exist with each new day to face!
But as we study carefully, forefathers true we find.
At Noah's birth, his father quoth: "This child will save mankind!"
And grandpa Enoch loved the Lord and didn't have to die;
The Bible says "He walked with God" who took him up on high!

Godly families help their sons a good life to afford,
So it was that Noah "found grace in the eyes of the Lord!"
No doubt his young wife suffered with agonizing fears,
But she firmly stood right by her man through all those awful years!
So while he preached and built the ark, they trusted in the Lord,
For God said He'd bring judgment, and they believed His Word!
Just one wife, it seems, he had, and through centuries of sin,
They raised three boys, they married wives. The ark – all entered in.

Then surely Mrs. Noah had her work cut out to do;
To care for all those animals, and feed her family too.
With birds and bears and bunnies, and fox and kangaroos;
Lions, elephants and cows, and everything by twos!
Then there were groups of sevens to sacrifice one day.
The ladies must have worked quite hard with little time for play!
Maybe their minds pictured that sweet garden there, and Eve!
Mrs. Noah knew the tale – likely longed for such reprieve!

But she loved her righteous husband, who through faith the ark had built,
And so she labored with him while the whole world died in guilt!
There were surely times of worry, and fear when thunder rolled,
But no doubt her husband's comfort, and his love her heart consoled.
And God, sparing all her family, would be a source of joy,
For the righteousness of Noah had reached each girl and boy!
This couple was due honor, as history's page unfurled,
For through their children's children, they would populate the world!

ABRAHAM & SARAH
"Love With A Promise"

*"And I will make of thee a great nation,
and I will bless thee, and make thy name great,
and thou shalt be a blessing."*
Genesis 12:2

Abraham and Sarah led a fulfilling life of faith. It was a life of excitement and adventure as they obeyed God and traveled far away from home and family.

The Patriarch - Abraham

What did God tell Abraham in Genesis 12:1?
_____
_____

What was seven-fold promise to Abraham if he obeyed God? Genesis 12:2-3

I will_____
I will _____
I will _____
You will _____
I will _____
I will_____
In you_____

What did Abraham do and how old was he when he received God's promise? Genesis 12:4_____
_____

Who and what did Abraham take with him? Genesis 12:5
_____
_____

When Abraham and his household arrived in the land of Canaan (v. 5) the Lord appeared to him once again. What Did he tell Abraham? Genesis 12:7a

_____

What did Abraham do when God told him that? Genesis 12:7b

_____

Altars were a symbol of worship and a reminder of God's faithfulness.

What does Hebrews 11:8-9 tell us about Abraham's faith?

_____
_____
_____
_____
_____

The Princess - Sarah

Can you even begin to imagine the thoughts going through Sarah's mind as they started on this journey of faith!

What does I Peter 3:3-6 tell us about Sarah?

_____
_____
_____

However, Sarah wasn't always submissive and she didn't always have a gentle and quiet spirit.

The Promise

Read Genesis 15:1-6 God gave Abraham another promise. What was it? (v. 4)_____

What was Abraham's response (v. 6) _____

_____

The Problem

Abraham and Sarah were getting up in years and Sarah was barren. Sarah got tired of waiting for God's promise to be fulfilled and took matters into her own hands.

What was Sarah's scheme to help God keep His promise? Genesis 16:1-3

_____
_____
_____

What happened that Sarah did not count on? Genesis 16:4-5

_____

Sarah sent Hagar away, but the Angel of the Lord found Hagar in the wilderness and told her to return to Sarah and submit to her. What happened in Genesis 16:15?

_____
_____

Although Hagar bore Abraham a son, Sarah's plan had not really worked because Ishmael was not the son of promise!

The Power

Abraham was now 99 years old and Sarah was 89. What did God tell Abraham? Genesis 17:15-16

_____
_____
_____

What was Abraham's reaction to this announcement? Genesis 17:17 _____

_____

_____

What did God tell Abraham once again in Genesis 17:19-20

_____

_____

_____

What did the Lord say to Abraham within the hearing of Sarah? Genesis 18:10

_____

_____

What was Sarah's reaction to the announcement and why? Genesis 18:12

_____

_____

_____

What question did God propose to them in Genesis 18:14a?

_____

What did God again promise to them? Genesis 18:14b

_____

God's power was proven to them in Genesis 21:1-2 What happened?

_____

_____

_____

_____

What did Sarah say? Genesis 21:6-7 _____
_____
_____
_____
_____

God's power is beyond our comprehension, and nothing is too hard for God!

What testimony does Hebrews 11:11 (KJV) give of Sarah?
_____
_____
_____
_____
_____

<u>*Looking upward to God*</u>

*** *God is Omnipotent* ***

He is strong and powerful enough to meet every situation in your life. Nothing is impossible with God.

Psalm 24:8 _____
_____
_____

Jeremiah 32:17 _____
_____
_____
_____
_____

We can always count on the promises of God even when things seem impossible to us. Promises such as:

*Delight yourself in the Lord, and He will
give you the desires of your heart*
Psalm 37:4

*Ask, and it will be given to you; seek, and you will find;
knock, and the door will be opened to you.*
Matthew 7:7

*Do not be anxious about anything, but in everything, by
prayer and petition with thanksgiving, present your
requests to God. And the peace of God, which transcends
all understanding, will guard your hearts and your
minds in Christ Jesus.*
Philippians 4:6-7

*If any of you lack wisdom, he should ask God,
who gives generously to all without finding fault,
and it will be given to him.*
James 1:5

*Fear not, for I have redeemed you,
I have summoned you by name; you are mine.
When you pass through the waters,
I will be with you; and when you pass through
the rivers, they will not sweep over you.*
Isaiah 43:1-2

*Therefore I tell you, do not worry about your life,
what you will eat or drink; or about your body,
what you will wear. Is not life more important
than food, and the body more important than clothes?
But seek first His kingdom and His righteousness;
and all these things will be given to you as well.*
Matthew 6:25, 33

*I am the Light of the world. Whoever follows
me will never walk in darkness,
but will have the light of life.*
John 8:12

From My Heart to Yours . . .

Abraham and Sarah were very prosperous in the city of Ur, a center of culture in Southern Mesopotamia. They had all the material things of life, plus family and friends nearby. Sarah was married to a man with strong convictions, and if she wanted to have a good marriage, she needed to adapt to Abraham's way of living and to a life of faith. This meant leaving a wealthy comfortable city where they complacently lived their lives, and becoming semi-nomads, traveling into the unknown, led by a God they could not see.

Let's think about it this way: What if your husband said to you, "Honey, we're going to move to a different country. God really spoke to my heart during my quiet time today and I feel He wants us to move on. God hasn't told me exactly where He wants us yet, but we're going to get on a plane and fly to a lot of different countries until God tells us we're in the right one. You can bring some of our things, but you can't bring everything. You'll have to decide what is most important to you. We'll have to visit everyone before we go because we don't know if we'll ever see them again. From now on, we're just going to walk by faith.

My husband and I became Christians when we were in our 30's. Within 3 years God had placed a desire in our hearts to go to Bible school. We were both earning good money, we had bought our 1st home - a beautiful two story colonial farmhouse that we had fixed up and redecorated, and we had two children in Christian school. Life was comfortable and good.

God wanted us to be willing to give all that up and follow Him. We quit our jobs, sold our home in NH and enrolled at Word of Life Bible Institute in upstate New York. It was amazing how God worked out all the details to get us there.

We had a yard sale and not only sold everything we had in the yard sale, but also sold our second car and our home that very day! We made enough money to pay tuition for ourselves at the Bible Institute, put our kids in Christian school, and pay all our expenses for the year (food, clothing, rent, books, etc) without having to work. What a great yard sale, and what a great God!!!

After graduating from the Bible Institute, God led us into full-time Christian work, working for Word of Life both in NY and FL. My husband then went on Pastoral Staff at our local church in FL before we retired. During that time God blessed us abundantly and we have so many great memories. Some of the blessings include going to Israel at no cost to us, discovering and using our spiritual gifts, and seeing people come to know the Lord through our ministry. We have been privileged to sit under the teaching of some of the greatest Bible teachers in the world, as well as some of the greatest musicians. We have made wonderful friends, and in recent years, God has called us into a writing ministry.

We have been married 52 years as of this writing and have grown together and become closer than ever before. It is God first, and then each other. Our prayer is to finish well.

Abraham and Sarah also had a happy ending in their marriage, and Sarah's life ended on a note of faith. She is the first woman recorded in Hebrews 11 where it speaks of the heroes of the faith.

*** *Marriage Wisdom* ***

Stand on the promises of God and not your own wisdom. Walk hand in hand with your mate and follow God wherever he leads.

Abraham and Sarah
by Jean Garner

Beyond the great Euphrates, in Ur of the Chaldees,
Lived Abraham and Sarah, in a land of wealth and ease.
With his father Terah and kith and kin to spare,
But grieved, perhaps, and saddened, by the evil worship there!
So Abraham was ready when the Lord to him did call:
"Get you out from here, God said, "and from your family – all!
I'll lead you to a far, strange land, and I will make you great!"
So heeding this divine command, in God's hand he placed his fate.

Father Terah died in Haran, so with Lot they journeyed on,
Carrying servants and possessions; 'twas a wealthy caravan.
And when he stopped at Shechem, he built an altar there,
When God appeared and told him: "Look about you everywhere.
Walk back and forth upon the land, and as far as you can see,
I bequeath to your descendants and I give this land to thee!"
And so God chose His people, and the Israel of today,
Looking back to Abraham, try to follow in his way!

He loved the Lord, did Abraham, but there were times to spare
When even he did wander from the Father's loving care.
He and Sarah, very old, still did not have a son,
And they were grieved and wouldn't wait for God to send them one!
So Sarah took upon herself to allow a "surrogate" wife;
And Ishmael, son of Abraham, has caused a world of strife!
But in God's ever perfect plan, son Isaac came to be
A type of God's own first-born Son, who came to set men free!

And on that awful, awful day, when Abraham took their son
To offer him a sacrifice - - Sarah's only one!
We wonder if she knew ahead what God commanded there?
If so, she must have spent those days in agonizing prayer!
But God does always what is best, for every precious child;
He had provided there, a ram, caught in brambles wild.
So Abraham learned, as so ought we, on Moriah's hill that day,
'Tis not just sacrifice God wants, but to trust and to obey!

ISAAC & REBEKAH
"Sweet Love That Soured"

"Do not be wise in your own eyes;
Fear the Lord and shun evil.
This will bring health to your body
And nourishment to your bones."
Proverbs 3:7-8

The beginning of Isaac and Rebekah's romance warms the heart. Everything goes smoothly and is so sweet that it's impossible to imagine anything going wrong with this couple. And yet, something went very wrong.

But first, let's look at the way it started out. Remember that Isaac was the son of promise, born to Abraham and Sarah in their old age. If ever a child was loved, it was he. Isaac grew and matured and was now at an age where he should be married. He was 40 years old and his mother, whom he loved dearly, had died. His father was concerned that Isaac have the right kind of bride

Read the romantic chapter of Genesis 24, and then go back and answer the questions.

The Mission – Genesis 24:1-6

What was Abraham's mission and why?_____

_____

_____

The Messenger – Genesis 24:2-4, 9-14

What information does verse 2 tell us about the messenger that Abraham chose for his mission?_____

_____

List everything you learn about the messenger's character from verses 9-14.

_____
_____
_____

The Method – Genesis 24:12-15

In one word, how did the messenger go about fulfilling his mission? _____

Proverbs 3:5-6 gives us a look at the method for any mission. Write out these verses and commit them to memory.

_____
_____
_____
_____
_____

The Maiden – Genesis 24:15-28, 57-61

How does verse 16 describe Rebekah?
_____

What do you learn about Rebekah's character from verses 17-28?_____
_____
_____
_____

What do you learn about her faith from verses 57-61?
_____
_____
_____

The Meeting - *Genesis 24:63-64*

Where did Isaac and Rebekah meet?
_____

What similar phrase in both verses stands out to you and why?
_____
_____
_____

This gives a whole new meaning to why we should "keep looking up!" ☺

The Marriage - *Genesis 24:67*

Write out verse 67:_____
_____
_____
_____
_____

This was a romantic beginning for two people in love. God brought them together as man and wife and they knew they were in the center of His will.

Now let's fast-forward 20 years. Rebekah did not bear children until she was 40 years old and Isaac was 60.

In Genesis 25:23 God gave Rebekah a promise. What was it?_____
_____
_____

The day came when the birth announcements could be sent out. Read Genesis 25:24-26 and fill in the birth announcement:

GENESIS 25:24-26

Announcing Twin Boys

Eldest: *Youngest:*

Details of birth:

Proud parents are:

Problems in the marriage began as the boys grew older. What does Proverbs 25:27 tell you about these men and their personalities?

Esau - _____

_____

Jacob - _____

What was the real problem? Genesis 25:28

_____
_____
_____

Read Genesis 25:29-34. What did Esau, the oldest boy do that showed he despised his birthright when he came home from the fields hungry and faint?

_____

And, in Genesis 26:34-35, Esau, at age 40, brought grief to his parents by marrying pagan girls.

Fast-forward again to when Isaac was old and his eyes were dim. Who did he call to his side and what did he say? Genesis 27:1-4

_____
_____
_____
_____
_____

Who overheard the conversation and how did she plot to deceive Isaac? Genesis 27:6-27

_____
_____
_____
_____
_____

What was the blessing Isaac bestowed upon Jacob, thinking he was Esau? Genesis 27:28-29

_____
_____
_____

(continued on next page)

_____
_____
_____
_____
_____

Even though Isaac had been deceived by his wife Rebekah and youngest son, the blessing he gave to Jacob lined up with God's promise "the elder will serve the younger!" God will use everything for good to accomplish His purposes.

<u>*Looking upward to God*</u>

**** God is Truth ****

He never lies or tries to deceive us. We can trust His Word.

Psalm 100:5 _____
_____
_____
_____

John 14:6 _____
_____
_____

From My Heart to Yours . . .

This story started out bathed in wise counsel and prayer and ended in deceit and regrets. How we need to nurture our relationship with God each day in order to stay within His will!

Isaac and Rebekah had 20 years to build their relationship with each other before they had a child, but something went wrong. It reminds me of a cartoon I once saw in a newspaper many years ago. Hagar the Horrible is coming back from some great conquest and his wife yells out "Who is it?" Hagar says triumphantly, "It's me! The man who swept you off your feet 20 years ago." To which his wife replies "Well beat it! I'm married now!" We laugh, but the truth is people change and get lazy in their relationships.

Rebekah and Isaac had a divided home. Instead of loving each other and bringing both of their children up in the nurture and admonition of the Lord, they each had their favorite child. Any unity, harmony or stability that might have been in their home dissolved. It was all downhill from there.

Rebekah tried to fulfill God's promise in her own wisdom and strength. This led to deceit and heartache. Like Sarah, when she gave her handmaiden to Abraham, Rebekah was trying to help God out, and in so doing, proved that she had little faith in His Word

Instead of going to her husband and having some meaningful communication with him about God's promise, and honoring him as the head of the home, she decided to totally side with Jacob against her own husband. What a far cry from their romantic beginning when Rebekah considered Isaac a gift from God and a part of God's will for her life.

In a race it's easy to start out good, but it's the person who runs the whole race according to the rules that eventually becomes the winner. Rebekah made her own rules; therefore, she lost!

Rebekah lost in many ways because of her deceit:
- Her children lost respect for her
- Her husband could not safely trust in her
- She caused Esau to hate his brother and desire to kill him. (Gen. 27:41)
- She had to send Jacob away to save his life, (Gen. 27:42-43) and she never saw him again because she died before he came back.

*** *Marriage Wisdom* ***

Be united in spirit and purpose with your mate, and train your children in the ways of God. Be creative in keeping the romance in your marriage.

Romance Enhancers

Loving - I Corinthians 13
Visualize an invisible sign around your mate's neck that says "Make me feel important and loved."

Learn the real meaning of love by studying I Corinthians 13. List the things that love does, the things that love is not, the things that love does not do. Then evaluate your love life, and with God's help, make some needed changes. This won't happen overnight, but if you stick with it, you and your mate will begin to see wonderful changes.

Cleaving - Genesis 2:24; Ephesians 5:31
Give up your dreams of a "perfect marriage" and work toward a good marriage.

Abandon all dependency on your parents and do not criticize his relatives. After God, your mate should be your main focus. Develop unity in as many areas as possible and discover new things to enjoy together. This will take work and perseverance.

Being Thankful - Ephesians 5:20; Philippians 2:14
Give praise and appreciation often

Keep a daily list of reasons to be thankful for your mate and greet him with affection, instead of nagging and complaining. Focus on the good he does and not his faults. Leave those to God.

Submission - Ephesians 5:21-24
Submit to him as unto the Lord and resist the temptation to be independent

Submission includes abandoning all hope of changing your husband through criticism or attack. And it means talking everything over with your husband and not making important decisions on your own.

Serving - Philippians 2:3-4
Discover your husband's personal and unique needs and try to meet them.

Release yourself from the "Princess" mindset where you feel you deserve to be pampered and catered to every moment. Be a handmaiden of the Lord.

More Romance Enhancers

Smile when you see him
Uphold him in prayer
Exercise to keep yourself looking good
Write him a poem
Buy him a romantic card
Bake his favorite dessert
Compliment him
Tell him why you love him
Read up on his hobby
Do a chore for him
Prepare his favorite meal
Update photos of the two of you
Take him out for breakfast
Work on a project together
Thank him for the things he does
Buy him a little gift
Learn more about him
Always kiss him goodbye
Always say "I love you"
Pray together
Always speak well of him

Isaac and Rebekah
by Jean Garner

Such a sweet and lovely story filled with fairy-tale romance,
But the meeting of this couple didn't happen just by chance.
Isaac was a special gift, who came right straight from God;
Surely there was not a child more loved than he was loved!
He missed his mother dreadfully, after she had died,
And Abraham decided, now – his son should have a bride!
He would not have him marry from the pagans living then,
But sent his servant far away – back to his own kin.
What a picture here for us (as the servant wends his way)
Of the Holy Spirit searching out Christ's bride, in this our day!

Eliezer paused one day, beside a foreign well
And waited as the maidens came, their pitchers there to fill.
Then the servant prayed to God that He would send the one,
The maid that he had chosen as a bride for Abraham's son.
And as he stood there watching, in his heart he could but pray,
When he saw this lovely maiden coming toward him on that day,
With her pitcher on her shoulder and her voice both low and sweet,
As she offered water from the well and a place to eat and sleep!
Then the servant thanked the Lord for answer to his prayer,
For this was Abraham's brother's kin – Rebekah – standing there!
She took him to her family, where he his errand told.
They rejoiced then, with Rebekah, who was soon to leave the fold!

And so this lovely maiden from a land so far away,
Packed all her belongings, and with servants – the next day
Journeyed toward the promised land, where she would meet her love;
And the glorious thing about it – the plan was from above!
Isaac, just to meditate, about the fields would roam,
When he beheld the caravan, as it carried his bride home.
As Rebekah came to meet him, 'twas love, surely, at first sight,
For if God does the choosing, then the choice is always right.
And one day soon, our Lord will come, and we, as His own Bride,
Will love Him then forever, and never leave His side!

MR & MRS POTIPHAR
"Unfaithful Love"

"Can a man scoop fire into his lap without his clothes being burned? Can a man walk on hot coals without his feet being scorched? So is he who sleeps with another man's wife; no one who touches her will go unpunished."
Proverbs 6:27-29

Millions of women watch soap operas each day. They are intrigued by the plots of unfaithfulness and lust. Many who are dissatisfied with their own marriages toy with the idea of having an affair to bring a spark of excitement into their lives.

God warns about this type of behavior in His Word, and nowhere is the warning more fully realized than in the story of the Potiphars. We're going to pretend this story is a soap opera and here is the script:

Scripture: Genesis 39

Setting: Egypt

Characters:

> P_____ - Complacent, leadership position, very well off. Meditates on career.

> P_____'s W_____ - Carnal, foolish, bold, immodest, selfish, unfaithful, idle. Meditates on Joseph.

> J_____ - Committed, godly, successful, deep convictions. Meditates on God's Word.

And then we have four scenes to this soap opera:

<u>Scene 1</u> - *She Looked* - Genesis 39:1-7
What did she see?

Do you think it is a sin to be tempted? Why or why not?

<u>Scene 2</u> - *She Lusted* - Genesis 39:7-10
Lust: a desire to satisfy some craving of the body
Self-control: control of one's emotions, desires or actions

What were Mrs. Potiphar's thoughts and behavior?

Why do you think Mrs. Potiphar did not practice self-control and kept after Joseph even when he refused her?

What different kind of conversation do you think she could have had with Joseph after he refused her?

Scene 3 - *She Lost* - Genesis 39:8-13
What did Potiphar's wife continue to do?

How do you think she felt when Joseph fled from her, leaving his garment in her hand?

How do you think Joseph felt?

Scene 4 - *She Lied* - Genesis 39:13-20
Why do you think Mrs. Potiphar lied about Joseph?

How would you have felt if you had done right and were thrown into prison because of it?

Although Joseph found himself in prison for doing right, God worked it for his good. He was finally freed and appointed second in command to Pharoah, and in a time of famine, he and his family feasted, but we never hear anything else about Potiphar's wife.

Now maybe you are thinking to yourself, 'Well, that makes a great soap opera, but I would never do something like that, so what has this to do with me?'

All sin is common to each one of us, and given the right set of circumstances and the right timing, we are all capable of committing any sin.

What does the Bible tell us in Galatians 6:1?

_____
_____
_____
_____

We can all be tempted. It is when we are complacent and prideful and sure of ourselves that Satan can come in and wipe out our testimony. We have an enemy who plays dirty because he hates us.

I Peter 5:8 describes our enemy:

_____
_____
_____
_____

Progression of Temptation - James 1:13-15

L_____ → S_____ → D_____

> *It is not a sin to be tempted. Only when you dwell on and give in to the temptation does it become sin. Jesus was tempted, but He did not sin.*

What does Proverbs 3:7 tell us?

_____
_____

What does II Timothy 2:22 advise us to do when faced with temptation? _____

Reasons we should not get involved in immorality

1. II Samuel 12:14 says that it causes the enemies of the Lord to _____.

   You could see how that would happen. You might be witnessing to an unsaved neighbor and then they hear of a preacher or teacher of God's Word who has fallen into immorality, or maybe even you, yourself. They say mockingly, "Sure Christianity is different. Tell me about it!"

2. Job 31:12 - It (meaning immorality) is a fire that _____ to _____ and would root out all your _____.

   Anything good you've built up in your life - a reputation, a ministry, leadership, self-image, family life - it can all be destroyed in a moment by immorality.

3. I Corinthians 6:13 says that the body is not for fornication, but it is for _____.

   You need to dedicate your body to the Lord to be used for His purposes, and not for any unrighteous acts. Just think of what it would be like to use your hands to serve God by helping others. To use your feet to walk in the light of God's Word. To use your mouth to praise God and build others up. To use your eyes to recognize needs. To use your ears to listen to someone who is hurting. To use your heart to be tender and sensitive to God and what He wants to accomplish in your life.

4. I Corinthians 6:18 - You are sinning against _____.

   We hurt ourselves more than anyone else.
   e.g. sexual diseases

5. I Thessalonians 4:3 says "It is the _____ that we abstain from fornication."

   Fornication: sexual misbehavior or impurity in any form

   It is never God's will for us to participate in pre-marital sex, adultery, homosexuality or pornography. God created sex for marriage between a man and a woman.

Satan tries to paint a beautiful picture of sin in our minds, but he doesn't show us the end result of guilt, shame, heartbreak and broken lives. He is out to destroy us!

What standards and safeguards do you have in place regarding the opposite sex? If you haven't thought about this before, think about it now and jot down some things that would be God-honoring. (Pray about this first and ask God for discernment)_____

_____
_____
_____
_____
_____

As a married woman, these are some of the standards and safeguards that I use in my life:
- Scripture Memory - so that the Holy Spirit can bring those verses to mind when I am tempted
- Not to flirt and use flattery
- To be modest in dress, actions and speech
- Not to be alone with men other than my husband
- Not overly physical (just a quick hug when appropriate)
- To be concerned about their relationship with God and not be a stumbling block
- To flee towards God when tempted

Do you think Potiphar's wife loved Joseph and wanted the best for him? Why or why not?

_____
_____
_____
_____
_____

Looking upward to God

> ### *** *God is Omnipresent* ***
>
> Everything is within God's view. There is nothing His eyes do not see. We cannot hide from Him.
>
> Proverbs 15:3 _____
> _____
> _____
>
> Psalm 139:12 _____
> _____
> _____
> _____

From My Heart to Yours . . .

The wife of Potiphar did not love either her husband or Joseph, but just wanted to satisfy her own desires

Let's think about the characteristics of Potiphar's wife so we can learn and examine our own lives for any traits that threaten to take us in the wrong direction.

Mrs. Potiphar was foolish
We know she was foolish because she didn't have the "fear of the Lord" which is the beginning of wisdom. She could have cared less about God and was ruled by her own lust. She totally disregarded Joseph's testimony.

At any point she could have turned to Joseph and said "Why are you so different? Tell me about your God." She could have turned to God in repentance and He would have forgiven her and made her a new person. But she never did.

Mrs. Potiphar was bold
She said outrageous things. She was fearless. She didn't care what God thought of her or what other people thought of her. She reminds me of women today who don't want to be known only as someone's wife - they want a name for themselves. They want the convenience of marriage, but they want to do their own thing.

There's a little bit of irony in this story because God doesn't even tell us her first name. She will always be known as Potiphar's wife.

Mrs. Potiphar was immodest
She was immodest in her speech, and most likely in the way she dressed. When she was trying to seduce Joseph

She probably wore something sexy that showed off her figure to the best advantage.

We need to be very careful about what we wear and what we allow our daughters to wear so that we will not defraud men. By immodest I'm talking about low necklines, see through clothing, halter tops, clothing that is skin-tight, immodest bathing suits, short-shorts, long slits, stiletto heels. Make it a project to prayerfully go through your closet with a discerning eye.

Mrs. Potiphar was selfish
She wanted to satisfy her own cravings instead of meeting needs in others. She knew Joseph was a man of God and yet she tried to bring him down to her level.

Mrs. Potiphar was unfaithful
There are a number of ways we can be unfaithful. Potiphar's wife was unfaithful to her husband. Ephesians 5 tells us to submit ourselves to our own husbands as unto the Lord, treating him with reverence and respect. Are you trying to do that?

Maybe you've never been physically unfaithful to your husband, but what about your thought life? Do you flirt with other men and think of what it might be like to be with them? This is a dangerous practice because of James 1:14. Remember: LUST → SIN → DEATH! If you allow yourself to think about sin, actions will eventually follow, and then spiritual death (separation of fellowship with God).

Christian women sometimes put their pastors and other men whom they perceive as spiritual on pedestals. When you put another man foremost in your mind, and your husband takes 2nd or 3rd or 4th place, you are putting yourself and your marriage in danger.

Sometimes you can be unfaithful in other ways as well. For instance, in your relationship with God. Do you obey Him?

Do you reverence Him? Do you meet with Him each day? Or do you put other people and things before Him?

What about faithfulness in your responsibilities? For example, do you know what your spiritual gift is and do you use it? Do you tell your friends and neighbors about Jesus? Do you train your children and grandchildren? Are you a keeper at home? Are you teaching younger women how to love their husbands?

If you determine you have any of the characteristics of Potiphar's wife in your own life, make a decision to submit yourself to God and ask Him to help you be the woman He wants you to be.

How to Overcome Lust -James 4:6-10

Even if you don't think you'll ever have a problem in this area, you will undoubtedly come across people who do, and maybe you will have opportunity to help them.

The key to these verses is found in verse 6 - HUMILITY! God resists the proud (don't be proud of your sin), but gives grace to the humble (confession of sin).

Therefore:

1. Submit Yourself to God (His Word)

    Put yourself under the authority of God's Word. Read it every day. Meditate on it. Think about it. Ask God to teach you and convict you. Obey what it says. Purpose in your heart to obey Him no matter what. Do it as an act of your will - the feelings will follow.

2. Resist the devil

    Memorize Scripture now that has to do with your sin so that you will have ammunition to defend yourself when Satan comes to tempt you. It is the Scripture that has the power - we have none. The Bible promises that Satan will flee from us, but we have to be ready. If we don't have the ammunition, Satan will defeat us. Although we can never lose the war as Christians, we can lose many battles and get hurt in the process.

3. <u>Draw Near to God</u>
Thank God for who He is, for what He can do, for what He has done. Love Him, appreciate Him, adore Him. Give Him credit for everything good in your life. Depend on Him in everything you do. Tell Him everything that is on your heart and ask for His help. As you draw near to God, He will draw near to you.

Part of drawing near to God is to:

<u>Cleanse your hands</u>
Stop doing what you used to do and stop wanting to do those things.

and <u>Purify your heart</u>
Think of sin the same way God thinks of it - as evil - something that nailed Christ to the cross. Hate sin. Be sad this thing is in your life and cry out to God to remove it. Be sad you are hurting and displeasing the Lord and be truly repentant.

Potiphar's wife thought it was in her best interests to chart her own course instead of learning about God and His commandments. She was completely deluded by Satan, and generations of people down through the ages have read about her foolishness. We must be very careful not to give the devil a foothold in our lives.

Humble yourself in the sight of the Lord and He shall lift you up. Again, the key is HUMILITY. Stop thinking of your sin as some little harmless character flaw and see it as something out to destroy you and your testimony. And when you flee temptation, be sure you don't leave a forwarding address.

There are many Christian leaders who have gotten involved in sexual immorality, and their ministries have been ruined. The Christian divorce and remarriage rate is steadily climbing out of control.

As women, we will be held accountable to God for how we conduct ourselves. We must purpose in our hearts not to ever be a part of the enemy's plan to destroy men's lives, and to cause the enemies of God to blaspheme.

Men are turned on by sight - we need to be careful of the scenery we are showing them.

Men are turned on by attitudes. We need to be careful about what we are harboring in our hearts. We need to be developing a humble and quiet spirit by submitting ourselves to God and to our own husbands as unto the Lord.

*** Marriage Wisdom ***

Invest your time and energy in loving God and your mate, and you will reap love and joy.

The grass may look greener elsewhere, but it's not. God expects us to be faithful

Mr. and Mrs. Potiphar
By Jean Garner

In the land of Egypt long ago, when Joseph was a slave,
The King's guard was Potiphar, a captain tall and brave.
He trusted Joseph with his house and all his business there,
For Joseph truly loved his God and spent much time in prayer.
The captain had a charming wife, selfish and spoiled it seems;
She cast her eyes on Joseph and dreamed her sensuous dreams.
Just like today's soap operas, she steadily made campaign
To seduce this handsome Hebrew, his affections she would gain!
But Joseph trusted in the Lord and held his morals high;
So when she made advances, he quickly passed her by.
But in her evil little heart, she lusted for this one;
For Joseph was a handsome lad and good to look upon!

So when her master was away, and no servant was within,
She caught Joseph by his garment, tempting him to sin!
But Joseph, having had enough, rebuked her there and then;
He would not bring dishonor upon his God or kin!
But when he quickly rushed away, she grabbed his garment then
And held it there to show her spouse when he came home again.
How very angry then she was – a blow to her great pride;
When the captain did come home, about Joseph then she lied!

But Joseph stood there straight and strong, he did not cringe or quail,
When Potiphar believed her lies and sent him off to jail.
He knew who would take care of him, his life was in God's hand:
There had to be a reason he was brought to this strange land!

But what of Mrs. Potiphar? Did she have a conscience then?
Deleted from God's manuscript – we don't hear of her again.
Did the Potiphars enjoy their life? We can but surmise,
For a foundation for a marriage cannot be built on lies!
The stories in God's Word, it seems, sometimes with sin are rife,
But God intends we learn from them, to live a better life!

NABAL & ABIGAIL
"Longsuffering Love"

"Strengthened with all might, according to His glorious power, unto all patience and longsuffering with joyfulness."
Colossians 1:11

Did you ever want something so bad, and then when you received it, it wasn't what you expected at all? Sometimes it's like that with marriage.

Many women are locked into a marriage with a difficult husband and think to themselves "Lord, wouldn't I be better off without this man? Surely you don't want me to remain in this situation! It just isn't fair!"

When we are in a difficult place, our thoughts tend to linger on our plight and we become discontent. God often allows His children to go through difficult times so that they might call upon His grace and be able to shine forth in the midst of darkness. He also uses our difficulties to help others who will have difficulties later.

Such is the story of Nabal and Abigail found in I Samuel 25.

The Personalities - I Samuel 25:2-3

How is Nabal described?_____
_____

Using a thesaurus, write down some synonyms for "churlish" or "surly."
_____
_____
_____

Doesn't Nabal sound like a real sweetheart? How would you like to sit across the breakfast table from him each morning?

Proverbs 2:12-15 gives us more insight into Nabal's character, as it describes the evil man. List things it says about him?

v. 12 _____
v. 13 _____
v. 13 _____
v. 14 _____
v. 14 _____
v. 15 _____
v. 15 _____

Before you begin thinking that Abigail must have been pretty weird to marry a guy like that, remember that in those days marriages were often arranged, and the women did not have much choice. Nabal was rich and this might have been why Abigail's parents arranged this marriage. Or maybe Nabal didn't show his true colors until after he married. But no matter what the reason, Abigail found herself in an unchangeable situation.

Abigail is described in I Samuel 25:3. What does it say about her?

_____
_____

Abigail means "*God gives joy*" which explains her beautiful countenance. She wasn't filled with bitterness and complaining as she viewed her circumstances for she realized that God was the source of her joy, not her husband. Perhaps her marriage forced her to seek God with her whole heart, and God was faithful to her.

What does Proverbs 2:11-12a tell us about what happens when we trust in God and not in our own wisdom?

_____
_____
_____

One of the big dangers of hanging around an evil person like Nabal all the time is that you could become like him (Proverbs 22:24-25), especially if you are bitter against God. Abigail could have become angry, irritable, arrogant and rebellious but instead she lived up to her name - "*God gives joy.*" She trusted in God regardless of the circumstances.

The Problem - *I Samuel 25:4-13*

Nabal was enough of a problem in day to day life, but then he caused an even bigger problem. David and his men had protected Nabal's shepherds and sheep from marauders and only expected some food in payment. It came to be sheep shearing time - a time of celebration for Nabal's servants for all the hard work they had done. David sent some of his men to make a request to Nabal that they be included in the festivities because of the part they had in the protection of Nabal's livelihood.

Nabal's answer was typical of his character. He said in verse 10a:_____
_____
(In other words, "Who does David think he is?")

The continuation of his answer in verse 11 shows his arrogance. Circle all the personal pronouns in this sentence:

> "Shall I then, take my bread, and my water, and my flesh that I have killed for my shearers, and give it unto men whom I know not whence they are?"

Instead of being thankful to God for his prosperity, Nabal took all the credit himself and selfishly held on to what he had. He wasn't about to share it with anyone.

What happened when David's men reported back to him what Nabal had said? I Samuel 25:12-13

_____

_____

David was a very angry man.

The Peacemaker - *I Samuel* 25:14-35

The servants came and reported to Abigail all that had happened and that David was very angry and out for revenge. (verses 14-17)

Abigail was used to dealing with an angry man and God had given her insight and wisdom into this turbulent emotion. She quickly had her servants prepare food for David and his men, and went the extra mile by going to meet them in person.

What does Proverbs 15:1 tell us?_____

_____

_____

What are the first three characteristics of God's wisdom in James 3:17?

_____

Abigail went to meet David, armed with God's wisdom in order to make peace. She was gracious and hospitable to him and her soft words charmed him and calmed him down. She appealed to his better (godly) nature

David's response was to praise God for sending Abigail.

For what two reasons was he thankful? I Samuel 25:33
_____
_____
_____

What were his parting words to her in I Samuel 25:35b?
_____
_____
_____

The Penalty I Samuel 25:36-38

Abigail went back home to find Nabal very drunk so she waited until the next morning to tell him all that had happened. What was Nabal's reaction to what Abigail told him? verses 37-38
_____
_____
_____

Write out the last part of Romans 12:19 _____
_____

In I Samuel 25:39 David praises the Lord for keeping him from taking his own revenge.

The Proposal - I Samuel 25:39-42

Write out the last sentence of verse 39
_____
_____

What was Abigail's response in verse 42? _____
_____
_____

Looking upward to God

*** *God is Faithful* ***

He will never leave us nor forsake us. He will be with us in good times and bad, and will help us to become like Christ. He will enable us to do His Will and He will finish the work He has started in us.

II Thess. 3:3 _____
_____
_____

I Peter 4:19 _____
_____
_____
_____
_____

From My Heart to Yours . . .

Contentment with the circumstances of your life, knowing that God is working in you, is a wonderful thing, and when you have it, you can relax and be at your best. There is nothing that robs a woman of beauty more than bitterness and complaining, and nobody likes to be around that type of person for very long.

We all run into situations in our lives we wouldn't have ordered had it been left up to us. Things we don't like to do, people we don't like to be with, problems we don't want to deal with. Disappointments and disillusionment. And yet God says we are to be happy when these things happen, because He is using them in our lives to build patience and endurance (James 1:3-4) as we submit ourselves to Him.

He promises in Romans 8:28 to work all things together for our good, and because He loves us and never breaks His promises, we can trust Him to do what He says.

We can learn to be content, knowing that God knows what we are going through, but knowing also that we need these things in our lives to mold us into the women He wants us to be. He wants us to be beautiful women, shining forth from the inside.

The main secret of contentment is to take life as it comes and make the best of it. In other words "***Bloom where you are planted***." This is a phrase I hope will stick in your mind.

Another secret of contentment is to have inward resources so that you are not dependent on, or at the mercy of outward events and circumstances. We need to develop greater faith in God and trust Him to complete the work He started in us.

To be content:

~ Realize that conditions are always changing, therefore you cannot be dependent upon them. You can be happy today and it could change tomorrow. Or sad today and it could change tomorrow.

~ Realize that what matters most is your relationship with God, whether you have the most glorious circumstances or the most miserable.

~ God only brings into your life things that are needed to make you more like Christ. He never gives you more than you can bear (I Cor. 10:3).

~ Realize that whatever God wills and permits is necessary and for your good because He loves you. That's what faith is all about - trusting God's heart even when we can't see His hand.

~ Realize that whatever your conditions might be at this present time, they are only temporary, and can never rob you of the joy and glory that ultimately await you with Christ. There is coming a day when we will have perfect eternal joy and gladness. We need to keep that perspective during the bad times.

~ The grass always looks greener elsewhere, but usually isn't because every life has troubles.

~ You need to sink your roots into your unchangeable situation and grow by God's grace into something beautiful for His glory.

Abigail could have turned bitter and rebellious and lost her beauty. Instead she learned from God how to:
    Develop her inner beauty - so much so, it showed on her countenance.
    Depend on God for her joy - she found there was no one else she could count on to be faithful.

> Deal with angry people – she had years of dealing with Nabal.
> Encourage and inspire others – Abigail inspired her servants, David and his men, and she is still inspiring us today.
> Display God's grace and power in her life – she was strong in an almost unbearable situation.
> Be a truly beautiful godly woman, inside and out.

Abigail humbled herself and acknowledged that her husband sinned against David. She took responsibility herself for his guilt. She gave David food and reminded him of the great plans God had for him. "David, you're going to be the next king of Israel. You have fought the Lord's battles and He has rewarded you. You have kept yourself from evil up until this time. Don't do something in anger that you might regret. Don't blow it, David! Let God be your avenger; don't take it upon yourself."

David was very impressed with this beautiful woman and recognized that God was working through her. He and his men left peaceably.

The rest of the story is a little bit like a fairy tale. God caused the arrogant Nabal to die, leaving Abigail free to marry David, the sweet psalmist of Israel. She had no regrets. She had done everything she could for Nabal and had grown in the process. Now she was free to marry once again, and she took the opportunity eagerly. Can you even begin to imagine the excitement in her heart! Her Prince Charming had come. Finally she was going to have a wonderful life.

But Abigail needed to know that God was faithful because the fairy tale ended almost as soon as she married David, for as we all know, life is not a fairy tale. Abigail would once again discover that her joy would have to come from the Lord because David would have many other wives, and he loved the beautiful Bathsheba most of all. Once again

Abigail found herself in circumstances that she wouldn't have chosen.

Abigail never did get satisfaction or lasting joy from her marriages. We cannot depend on others, or on circumstances for our joy - only on God. Everyone and everything else will fail us at some point, but God never fails. He is our faithful God.

I like to think of Abigail being a counselor to other women. As they came to her for help in trials or sorrow, she could tell them with full assurance that God is faithful. That He could give joy in the worst circumstances. That He would help them through anything and give them purpose and dignity.

Her husband, David, wrote many beautiful psalms and I can imagine Abigail taking them as her own and praying to the Lord:

> *"The Lord is my strength and my shield;*
> *My heart trusts in Him, and I am helped.*
> *My heart leaps for joy and I will give thanks*
> *to Him in song.*
> Psalm 28:7

> *"Because You have been my help,*
> *I sing in the shadow of Your wings"*
> Psalm 63:7

Abigail learned to *"Bloom where she was planted"*. May God help each of us to do the same.

*** Marriage Wisdom ***

Work through the difficulties of your marriage with a joyful, humble spirit, knowing that God is working in you to make you more like Christ.

Abigail and Nabal
by Jean Garner

A fool by name and nature – and Nabal was his name;
Who only loved his worldly goods, and had plenty of the same.
"As is his name, so is he," is what his wife had said,
And there were times, no doubt, she would rather have been dead!
Nabal was a 'beast' for sure, but 'Beauty' too, was here;
The Bible calls her Abigail, a lady wise and dear.
Endowed with charm as well as brains; throughout her married life
No doubt she oft must intercede, to keep back war and strife!
You'd wonder how these two had met, and why they would have wed;
But parents often made the plans, and nothing could be said.
For he was rich with sheep and goats, and many servants, too;
But Abigail kept trust in God – what else was there to do?

David, with six hundred men, a motley, loyal band,
Was hiding in the rocks and caves, with little food on hand.
They drove away marauders and protected folk near by,
And in return, expected food and things they could supply.
But when they came to Nabal to ask a boon of him,
He railed on them and drove them out. Said: "Don't come here again!"
David was so angry, he gathered up his men,
And said: "We'll kill the scoundrel, and all his house and kin!"
A servant rushed to Abigail to see what she could do,
For though they hated Nabal, they loved their Mistress, true!

She made haste with cakes of figs and sheep and corn and wine
To carry them to David, and hoped she'd be in time
To avert retaliation by David and his men.
She fell at David's feet and begged forgiveness then
For her wicked husband, and said: "Put up your sword;
Use it only when you fight the battles of the Lord.
I know that thou art blessed of Him and soon will be the King
And now accept, I pray thee, these offerings that I bring!"
Abigail went home and told her husband, with some dread!
He promptly had a heart attack – in ten days he was dead!
Much impressed, was David, with the way she lived her life;
So very shortly after, Abigail became his wife.

DAVID & BATHSHEBA
"Love With Regrets"

"If you confess your sin, God is faithful and just to forgive you your sin and cleanse you from all unrighteousness."
I John 1:9

This story begins with two people in the wrong place at the wrong time. And that's how most sin starts.

He Stayed – II Samuel 11:1

According to II Samuel 11:1, where should David have been? Where was he?

_____
_____
_____

Why do you think it is important to be where God wants us to be, doing what He wants us to do?

_____
_____
_____
_____

He Saw – II Samuel 11:2

Because David was not where he was supposed to be, and was bored, what was Satan able to tempt him with?
_____

What happens when we do not turn our eyes away from temptation?_____
_____

What lesson could David have learned from Job 31:1?
_____
_____

David's first reaction to Bathsheba was lust. What does James 1:14 tell us?
_____
_____
_____

Why do you think modesty is important, even when we're in our homes?_____
_____
_____

He Summoned – II Samuel 11:3

What is the first thing David did after he saw Bathsheba?
_____

In doing this, he did not resist the temptation, but drew closer to it.

He Sinned – II Samuel 11:4-5

What happened because David did not turn to God for help in this moment of lust and temptation?
_____
_____

In what ways was David being selfish?_____
_____
_____
_____
_____

What do the following verses tell us about why we can't ever blame God for our temptations and sin:

James 1:13 _____
_____
_____

II Peter 2:9a _____
_____

What does God promise in I Corinthians 10:13? _____
_____
_____
_____

He Slew – II Samuel 11:6-17

What did David do in order to try and cover up his sin?
_____

He sorrowed – II Samuel 11-18

God's prophet, Nathan, came and told David that he had sinned in the sight of God and that there would be consequences. David is sorrowful and this is when he wrote the great 51st Psalm of repentance. And although God forgave David for his sin when he repented of it, he and Bathsheba still had to face the consequences of their sin of adultery. This chain of events would bring bitter trials and sorrow to their lives and to the lives of those closest to them.

II Samuel 11:5 - an illegitimate child
II Samuel 11:14-15 - murder of Uriah
II Samuel 12:14-19 - Bathsheba's child dies
II Samuel 13:8-14 - David's son Ammon rapes his half sister Tamar
II Samuel 13:23-34 - David's son Absalom murders Ammon

II Samuel 15:12,31 - David's counselor turns against him
II Samuel 15:13-14 - David had to flee from his son Absalom who wanted to kill him
II Samuel 16:21-22 - Absalom slept with David's concubines
II Samuel 18:15 - David's son Absalom was killed

Because of David's deep repentance, God gave tangible evidence of his forgiveness. Write out II Samuel 12:24:

_____
_____
_____
_____

Looking upward to God

*** *God is Forgiving* ***

When we are sorry for our sin and desire to turn from it, God is faithful to forgive us and to restore us to fellowship with Him.

Psalm 34:18 _____
_____
_____
_____

Proverbs 28:13 _____
_____
_____
_____

From My Heart to Yours . . .

David and Bathsheba's love affair has been the talk of Bible readers down through the ages, and their story was even portrayed in a Hollywood epic production.

They were two of the beautiful people - money, prestige, looks and fame. David was a king and used to getting what he wanted. He was beloved by his people and was called the "Sweet Psalmist of Israel." Bathsheba was the beautiful wife of Uriah, one of David's mighty and valiant fighting men.

Their paths crossed in a dramatic and passionate way, and the world would say "Go for it - you owe it to yourselves - grab love while you can." But God's love is not selfish, it does what is best for the other person. And adultery is never best.

David spent a lot of time weeping and regretting what he did. He was called a man after God's own heart because he sorrowed deeply over sin. Bathsheba was loved by David, but she too suffered in the loss of her first baby, and then the agony of watching her husband suffer so.

Although they did not escape the consequences of sin, God was merciful to them in giving them another child named Solomon. Solomon was the bright spot in their lives, and God promised them that Solomon would be king after David. I imagine much time was spent in acquainting Solomon in the ways of God.

Although Bathsheba is certainly not to be compared to Potiphar's wife, this story proves that we all have the potential to fall into adultery if the circumstances and timing are right.

As women, we must prepare our hearts for those temptations so that they do not catch us by surprise.

How do we do that? Psalm 119:11 tells us:

> *"Thy word have I hidden in my heart,
> that I might not sin against thee."*

When tempted by Satan, Jesus was victorious by using God's Word. And that is also the only way we will be victorious over temptation. If Bathsheba had hidden God's Word in her heart, she could have made a wiser decision when she was summoned by King David.

Can you think of any verses in Scripture that would have helped Bathsheba make a wiser decision when she was summoned by King David? If you can't, you won't be prepared when Satan comes to tempt you.

If you have even thought of adultery in your heart, ask God's forgiveness and ask Him to help you renew your mind through His Word. We should be able to say with David in Psalm 139:23-24:

> *"Search me, O God, and know my heart;
> Try me, and know my thoughts,
> and see if there be any wicked way in me,
> and lead me in the way everlasting.*

Again, let me remind you that we have an enemy out to destroy us. Satan knows that he is going to lose in the end, and wants to take as many of us down with him as he can. He wants to make us useless for God, and often he does that in the area of adultery.

Sin is something that a person can't blame on anybody but themselves. It's a matter of constant, willful choices. And because each choice we make builds on the previous one, it draws us either closer to God or further away.

> **A choice made often enough becomes a habit.**
> **A habit reaps a personality.**
> **A personality reaps a character.**
> **A character reaps a destiny.**

Someone once said, you can live your life any way you want, but:

> You can only live it once
> You have no control over the consequences of your actions
> You either pay for your choices ahead of time by self-discipline, or afterwards with regret.
> Your choices effect not only you, but also the people around you.
> Your choices will either bring you commendation or condemnation from the Lord.

Here are some tests you can give yourself to determine right or wrong choices:

Personal Test – Will doing it make me a better or a worse Christian?

Social Test – will doing it influence others to be better or worse Christians?

Practical Test – will doing it likely bring desirable or undesirable results/

Universal Test – suppose everyone did it?

Scriptural Test – is it expressly forbidden in the Word of God?

Stewardship Test – will doing it involve a waste of God's entrustment to me?

Missionary Test – will doing it likely help or hinder the progress of the Kingdom of God.

God promises in Psalm 32:8 that He will instruct you and teach you in the way you should go and guide you with His eye. In Philippians 1:10 "that you may approve things that are excellent."

Instead of continuing to listen to the enemy when he comes to tempt you in an effort to destroy your life, turn to God and ask Him for wisdom, strength and power to make the right choices.

WHAT SIN WILL DO FOR YOU

* **Sin** will take you further than you want to go.

* **Sin** will keep you longer than you want to stay.

* **Sin** will cost you more than you want to pay.

* **Sin** will cause you more guilt, grief and heartache than you can imagine.

"Guard your heart with all diligence, for out of it are the issues of life."
Proverbs 4:23

*** Marriage Wisdom ***

It is better to confess sin and ask forgiveness, than to try and cover it up and lose God's blessing on your marriage. But it's even better if you ask for God's help beforehand to resist temptation.

David and Bathsheba
by Jean Garner

David was a mighty man and God's own choice as King.
He warred with nations round about, great victories, to bring.
When battles there were in array, then David led his men,
And not till total victory, did they all come home again!
But one Spring David did not go to be at battle's head;
He sent his men with Captain Joab, to lead them in his stead;
And as the story then unfolds, a lesson here we see;
Wrong things happen if we're not where God would have us be.
So David, being bored, it seems – walked out into the night
And strolling on the palace roof, beheld a neighbor's light.
There across the roof tops, he eyed the lighted path
That showed Uriah's lovely wife, at her evening bath.
He summoned then Bathsheba – had a servant bring her in
And thus did David turn from God, and sin his greatest sin;
For following this was murder: Uriah's place he's filled,
So he sent him to the battlefront – made sure that he was killed!
He repented deeply of his sin, though to the end of days
David and his people suffered many untold ways.
He took Bathsheba as his wife, but when their son was born,
God made their baby very sick, which left them both forlorn.

God petitioned Nathan to come before the King,
And tell him then a story – righteous anger it would bring.
He told him of a poor man with one wee lamb – a ewe.
The two had grown together – just as his child would do.
Then there was a rich man, with flocks and herds galore;
And lo! One day a visitor appeared before his door.
He wished to make a feast for him, but not his sheep he slew;
Instead, he took the poor man's pet – the cuddly little ewe,
And had it killed and dressed and made into a feast;
That it broke the poor man's heart – he cared not in the least!

David was so angry! Said "I'll kill him if I can!"
But Nathan said, in solemn words: "David, you're that man!"

The Lord is much displeased, but to forgive – He'll not deny;
You'll suffer sore for all your sins. Bathsheba's child will die!"
This was just the first of many trials there would be,
But God still loved this wayward son – in future He could see
Another child born to these two – much happiness he brings,
For Solomon began the line – straight to the King of Kings!

MR & MRS JOB
"A Painful Love"

*"The Lord gave and the Lord has taken away,
may the Name of the Lord be praised."*
Job 1:21

When young couples stand before the altar and make their marriage vows to each other, I wonder if they really realize what they are saying, and if they've purposed in their hearts to keep those vows no matter what.

*"For better, for worse, for richer,
for poorer, in sickness and in health"*

These are awesome and sobering words if taken seriously, and if we lived up to them, we would be showing forth God's unconditional love to the world.

It's easy to have faith and love when things are going well and there's a steady paycheck coming in. But what happens when health fails, tragedy comes, and everything is going wrong? Would you then be a loving, faithful marriage partner, looking to God for strength?

<u>*In Good Times*</u> – Job 1:1-5

"For better, for richer, and in health"

Mrs. Job must have been a woman who was envied by everyone. She was married to a godly, prosperous, famous man who was respected. She had a life of luxury and ease and did not lack for anything.

Looking at Job 1:1-5, list some of the blessings Mr. & Mrs. Job had._____

_____

_____

Even though Job was very blessed, he did not hoard all his blessings for himself but shared with others. Job 29:12-17 talks about the people and projects Job was involved with and all the good he was able to do in his community. What were some of these things?

_____
_____
_____
_____
_____

Job was no hypocrite when it came to his faith in God. What does James 1:27 tell us about his faith?

_____
_____
_____

In Bad Times – Job 1:6-12

"For worse, for poorer, and in sickness"

While Mr. & Mrs. Job were living their good life here on earth, something was going on in Heaven they didn't know anything about.

Satan told God that Job only loved God because God had blessed him so much. God allowed Satan to take away whatever he wanted from Job in order to test Job's faith and to bring him even closer to God.

According to Job 1:13-19, what blessings of God were taken from Mr. and Mrs. Job?

_____
_____

In an instant, everything Job had worked for all his life was gone.

What was Job's reaction to all this in Job 1:20?

_____
_____
_____

What words came out of Job's mouth during this devastating time of loss? Job 1:21

_____
_____
_____
_____

It is obvious by Job's reaction that he spent time with God each day learning to trust in Him. Job's heart was prepared for this adversity.

As if this wasn't enough, we find Satan once again accusing Job before God. In chapter 2 Satan accuses Job of loving God only because he still has his health. So God allows Satan to attack Job's health, but not take his life.

What did Satan do to Job in Job 2:7?

_____
_____

When God allowed Satan to take away Job's health, how did his wife react in Job 2:9?

_____
_____

Even though Job was grieving and now had serious painful health issues, how did he respond to his wife in Job 2:10?

_____
_____
_____

Mrs. Job, in her nice comfortable little world, didn't know she would be facing great trials and sorrow ahead, and was not prepared for it because she did not have a close relationship with God. She had a faulty understanding of both God and Satan.

What a disappointment Job's wife must have been to him, when instead of comforting him with kind and gentle words, and praying with him and for him, she instead turned her back on God and saw their life as a hopeless situation.

And Job's friends weren't much better. They added to his already overwhelming agony by giving cold and hollow sermonettes, by offering heartless words of advice, and even by making unfounded accusations. After such a display, Job answered and said what in Job 16:2?

_____

_____

May God help us not to be "Miserable Comforters."

At this point, Job could have given up in despair. He could have wasted away in bitterness against God, his wife and his friends. Instead, he sought God's wisdom in dealing with these hard trials, and therefore was able to hold together his life, his marriage and his faith.

Painful experiences cause growth in our lives, and as a result of Job's suffering, He knew God in a way he had never known before.

When these trials were over, God gave Job twice as much as he had before. What were some of these things according to Job 42:10-12?

_____

_____

_____

_____

In Job 42:13 God even blessed Mr. & Mrs. Job with 7 more sons and 3 more daughters. In the resurrection his first ten children will be raised from the dead and will spend all eternity in Heaven with their mother and father and 10 new siblings. God truly did bless job with twice as much as he had before.

Looking upward to God

**** God is Sovereign****

He is in control and nothing comes into the life of a child of God that God does not allow. And if He allows it, He will work it for our good.

Proverbs 21:1 _____
_____
_____
_____

Romans 8:28 _____
_____
_____
_____
_____

From My Heart to Yours...

Perhaps you are going through a season of suffering and struggle with the realization that God is allowing it. Suffering is common to all, and if we do not prepare ourselves, we can turn into bitter, resentful people.

Suffering can help to purify us and to strengthen our character. No-one likes to think about going through suffering, yet when it is over, most people will tell you it was worth it because it brought them closer to God and made them more like Christ. They appreciate life more and they have their priorities straight. There is nothing like suffering to weed out the things that are not important.

There are many reasons for suffering, but no matter what the reason, it is the time to draw near to our loving God.

Sometimes we suffer because:

1. It is a natural result of growing old.
   The elderly suffer from physical pains and poor health, mental anguish, regrets and loneliness.

2. It is a natural result of continued sin. Galatians 6:7 We reap what we sow. If we sow to the flesh, we reap corruption.

3. Of sin at a particular point in our lives. I Corinthians 11:30 "For this cause, many are weak and sickly among you, and many sleep (die)."

4. It can be used to prevent sin in our lives. II Corinthians 12:7-10 Paul had his thorn in the flesh; a weakness that God was able to show His strength through. God might allow suffering in our lives at intervals for the purpose of keeping us humble,

especially if He plans to use us in a great way.

5. Suffering is a form of discipline and chastisement. Hebrews 12:5-7
   This does not mean punishment. God does not punish us because Christ bore the punishment for all of our sins on the cross. But instead, it means training. God loves you and is seeking to change your behavior. He knows what behavior will hurt you and seeks to take it from you.

6. God chooses suffering to bring glory to Himself. John 9:1-3; John 11:4

   John 9:1-3 is the story of the man blind from birth. The disciples asked Jesus if it was because of sin. Jesus answered and said "Neither has this man sinned, nor his parents, but that the works of God should be made manifest in him. Jesus healed this man and at the end of the chapter, the blind man was saved. This, of course, brings glory to God.

   John 11:4 tells us that when Lazarus was sick, Jesus said "This sickness is not unto death, but for the glory of God that the Son of God might be glorified by it." Jesus raised Lazarus from the dead. John 11:45 says that "many of the Jews who came to Mary, and had seen the things that Jesus did, believed on Him." Souls were added to the Kingdom of God because of suffering on the part of Lazarus and his family.

7. To open previously closed doors. e.g. Joseph, Moses)
   Can you imagine the suffering Joseph went through when his brothers grabbed him and threw him in a pit and then sold him as a slave? Can you imagine the suffering he went through when he was thrown into prison because of the lie of Potiphar's wife? There is also the suffering of Joseph's father when

he thought his son had been devoured by animals. Yet God had a plan, and in a time of famine, Joseph was able to feast along with the rest of his family in Egypt where he was 2nd in command.

And then Moses. The anguish his parents must have felt having to give him up and knowing that he was being brought up in an Egyptian palace instead of their home. But God was preparing a leader for His people, to lead them out of bondage, and this called for a certain amount of suffering. God might have a plan for later on in our lives that causes us to suffer now.

8. Suffering can cause growth in our lives. Job 42:1-6; Psalm 77; 119:67,75-76
   As a result of suffering, we can know God in new and deeper ways.

9. Suffering gives God the opportunity to comfort us. Job 36:15; II Corinthians 1:3-4
   God is the God of all comfort, and He comforts us in all of our tribulation.

10. Suffering gives us the opportunity to comfort others. II Corinthians 1:4-8
    Before we suffer ourselves, we do not have the capacity to enter into another's sorrow and suffering. We tend to be judgmental and critical, and suffering gentles us.

11. Suffering helps us not to trust in ourselves, but in God. II Corinthians 1:9-10
    Suffering builds and proves our faith. Instead of being self-confident, we develop confidence in God.

12. We can give thanks for God's loving sovereignty in our lives and thanks may also be given by others who have prayed for us. II Corinthians 1:9-11

God loves to prove Himself to us and also to hear praise from His people.

13. We can enter in and experience the fellowship of His suffering. Philippians 3:10; I Peter 4:12-13
Christ suffered and bled and died for us that we may have eternal life.

The great question to ask in time of affliction is not "Why?", but "What?" What lesson does the Lord want me to learn in the midst of it all?"

As Christians, we should know that no experience in life can ever touch us except by permission of the Lord Himself. It is He who allows us to be tested, but never beyond what we are able to bear. Whatever God permits to touch our lives, we can be sure that He will bestow the power to see us through. We don't like to suffer, but we can at least know that God will work it for our good.

We should take a moment here to talk about not being a "miserable comforter."

A sufferer doesn't want a mere word of counsel or a sermon of sympathy, or even a well-known verse of Scripture. What a sufferer wants and needs is someone who will listen instead of talk, someone who will do, instead of giving advice.

When we do talk, how do we comfort people? What can we say that will make a difference? What things should we avoid saying? Let me just give you a few examples.

AT A FUNERAL
    Say: "I'll always remember (name)." Or, "I'll come by with dinner tonight."

    Don't say: "He's so much better off in Heaven." Or, "If there's anything I can do, call."

WHEN A BABY HAS DIED

<u>Say</u>: "I know how much being a mother means to you."

<u>Don't say</u>: "You can always have another one." Or, "At least you never got to know it."

ABOUT DIVORCE

<u>Say</u>: "The future must seem frightening. I'll stay close." Or, "I'm sure this is a lonely time for you. Let's have lunch."

<u>Don't say</u>: "I never liked the way he treated you." Or, "There are two sides to every story."

WHEN A PET DIES

<u>Say</u>: "I know she was important to your family."

<u>Don't say</u>: "It's only a dog! You can always get another one."

DURING TERMINAL ILLNESS

<u>Say</u>: "How are you feeling about what you are facing?" Or, "I'll take you to your next doctor's appointment."

<u>Don't say</u>: "I know a lady who had the same thing." Or, "Won't you be glad to be with the Lord?"

God wants His people to comfort His people. In Isaiah 40:1 He exhorts: "Comfort, comfort my people. These are my people; comfort them for me." In Isaiah 66:13 He says "As a mother comforts her child, so will I comfort you."

*** *Marriage Wisdom* ***

Trust God in all circumstances, and let your joy be anchored in God and not possessions.
Cling to God and each other during the tough times of life.

Mr. and Mrs. Job
by Jean Garner

We wonder why the trials come – why God allows the pain!
He could have many reasons, but we're sure it's for our gain.
It could be from a natural cause, or come from sin or shame,
Or He might just allow it, to bring glory to His name!
Perhaps to help us sympathize with others in their loss,
And bring us closer fellowship with Jesus on the cross.
We may not know the reason here, but some day we will know
Beyond a shadow of a doubt why we suffer here below!

And when we think of suffering and trials on this globe,
Our minds go back to ancient days, and to God's servant Job!
He was a great man of his time, with children, wealth and gold.
Neighbors gave him great respect, this patriarch of old.
Mrs. Job, no doubt – was envied by her friends;
The wife of such a rich man, and all that that portends.
Can't you envision her fine house with servants everywhere;
Her every wish was their command; they gave her greatest care!

We will not question ways of God – He knows what He's about,
Even though, some things He does, we cannot figure out!
One day God let Satan take Job's wealth and children, too;
"And now you'll see," He said to God, "Job surely will curse You!"
But he was wrong! Though in distress, Job uttered this wise word:
"God gives and God can take away. I still will bless the Lord!"
Satan still accuses Job – God allows him one thing more!
To cover him with painful boils – his body one huge sore!

Job still kept his faith in God, but heard his wife's shrill cry:
"How can you still stay true through this? I say – curse God and die!"
His wife was not much help to him in time of his distress.
He said: "God sends good as well as bad, so don't talk foolishness!"
Job's three friends then came to help. Poor comforters were they!
They declared, because Job sinned – disaster struck that day!
But God who honors men of faith, restored Job's life once more;
Gave again a family – doubled wealth he had before.
It seems there is a lesson here, God would have us know;
Keep faith in God no matter what our trials here below!

HOSEA & GOMER
"Unconditional Love"

"For I am persuaded that neither death, nor life, nor angels, nor principalities, nor powers, nor things present, nor things to come, nor height, nor depth, nor any other creature, shall be able to separate us from the love of God, which is in Christ Jesus, our Lord"
Romans 8:38-39

The story of Hosea and Gomer is a sad, but beautiful story of unconditional love. The love of one partner for another, without thought of getting anything in return, and regardless of how the object of that love responds back.

Unconditional love is faithful and loyal, always seeking the other person's good, no matter what! It is a supernatural love, always thinking of what it can give, instead of what it can get.

In these days of little commitment, divorce, and remarriage, it is refreshing and poignant to read of Hosea's love for Gomer, his wayward wife. And even more refreshing is the fact that God feels this type of love for His children. Nothing we can ever do as one of God's children, can cause God to separate Himself from us permanently. He will always be there waiting for us to turn from our sinful ways.

We find an example of God's unconditional love in the story of the Prodigal son in Luke 15:11-24. The son asked for an early inheritance and left home to pursue a party lifestyle. When his money ran out, he came to the end of himself, and was filled with remorse and shame. Knowing that he needed to return home, he wasn't sure how he would be received by his father.

How did his father react to his homecoming? Luke 15:20?
_____
_____
_____

What happens in Luke 15:22-23?_____
_____
_____
_____
_____
_____

The prodigal son was restored to full fellowship with his father, and in verse 24 the father tells why he is so happy to see his wayward son return home:_____
_____
_____

Ephesians 2:4-6 speaks of the love of our Heavenly Father for His wayward children, and puts us in the same category as the prodigal son. What do these verses tell us?
_____
_____
_____
_____
_____
_____

Gomer is cast in the role of the "Prodigal Wife." Hosea, who represented God to the nation of Israel, was about to learn through a very hard life experience just how much God loved His people. Hosea and Gomer were about to become a living object lesson of God's love.

Background

Hosea was a prophet during the reign of Jeroboam II. They were prosperous years, but the children of Israel had committed adultery against God by becoming involved with the false god, Baal. Through the adulterous acts of his wife, Gomer, Hosea's personal experiences became an object lesson of God's experience with Israel.

The story teaches that God suffers when His people are unfaithful to Him, but He will never cease loving His own, and seeks to woo them back into fellowship with Himself.

The Marriage

God tells Hosea to take a wife. What did Hosea do? Hosea 1:3 _____

_____

The names of all Gomer's children have significant meaning.

1st child - verse 4   Name: _____

    Meaning: "Scattered" (A reminder that God's judgment was coming)

2nd child - verse 6   Name: _____

    Meaning: "Not loved" (God would no longer show mercy to the nation of Israel because of their sin)

3rd child - vs 8-9   Name: _____

    Meaning: "Not my people" (Israel would turn far away from God)

As each child was born and Hosea began to ponder the meanings of their names, He realized that his wife was committing adultery and that their 2nd and 3rd child were probably not his children. Finally, she left him and pursued her lovers openly.

Describe how you think Hosea felt during this time:
_____
_____

Because this marriage is an allegory of God's experience with Israel, we begin to have some small insight of how God hurts when His children sin.

According to the following Scripture verses, what were the penalties for adultery?

       Leviticus 20:10   _____

       Leviticus 21:9   _____

       John 8:3-5   _____

Hosea could have demanded any one of those penalties for Gomer. Instead God empowered Hosea to show forth unconditional love to Gomer. No matter how far her heart was from him, he still loved and cared for her, hoping that she would return to him.

Many marriages today suffer because of the sin of adultery. Pride and self-pity rear their ugly heads, and the one sinned against discards their sinning partner because the world says "You don't deserve that kind of treatment. Get rid, of him and find yourself someone better."

As Christians, we need to realize that God does not want us to judge or be defeated by bitterness - He wants us to be part of the restoration process.

Write out Ephesians 4:32_____
_____
_____
_____

Write out Galatians 6:1 _____
_____
_____
_____

What are some of the things God forgave you for when you became a Christian?
_____
_____

Have you been completely faithful to God since you've been a Christian? In what ways have you failed?
_____
_____

We fail God each day of our lives and don't deserve His love. Yet God continues to love us and to encourage us to do better. It is His loving kindness and the security of His love that eventually makes us want to be pleasing to Him and to love Him in return. If God just cast us away when we sinned against Him, there would be no hope. But we have that wonderful promise in I John 1:9:
_____
_____
_____

What promise does Philippians 1:6 give us? _____
_____
_____

With the strong love of one marriage partner, it is possible to save the marriage, and even make it better than it was before.

Luke 1:37 _____
_____

Philippians 4:13 _____
_____

You must erase the word "divorce" from your vocabulary and be committed to saving your marriage. This means putting away pride, and developing a gentle, quiet spirit. It will mean giving 100% of yourself without expecting anything in return. It will mean hard work.

Write out Ephesians 4:2 _____
_____
_____

Gomer sunk so low that she ended up on the auction block, and the bidding was low. When we're a slave to sin, we're always auctioned off cheap, because when we are wallowing in the mud of this world, it is difficult for others to evaluate our worth.

Hosea, after years of heartbreak and embarrassment over his wayward wife, redeemed her from the slave market of sin and took her home. Gomer did not deserve it for she was a wicked woman, but Hosea had the unconditional love of God instilled in his heart for Gomer. He was able to love her and forgive her and restore her as his wife.

Write out the following verse to learn more of the unconditional love of God.

Romans 5:8 _____
_____
_____
_____

What does God's loving-kindness cause us to do? Psalm 63:3 _____

We are to try to show forth love in all situations, even in the case of an unfaithful marriage partner. When the people saw that Hosea was kind and tender toward Gomer, they listened afresh to his message from God.

I John 4:8 _____
_____

I John 4:11 _____
_____

Looking upward to God

**** God is Love ****

God always does what is best for us. As a child of God, you can feel secure in His love because He'll always bring you good and not evil. Nothing can ever separate you from His love.

Jeremiah 31:3 _____
_____
_____

Psalm 103:4 _____
_____
_____

From My Heart to Yours . . .

For this section I will share with you a story written by Dr. John W. Reed. It touched my heart so much and made me realize how far I was from expressing God's sacrificial love on a day to day basis. Enjoy!

I have been called the prophet of the broken heart, but I would rather be remembered as the prophet of love and hope. I am Hosea, prophet of God to Israel, my homeland.

We are standing in the front of my home in the outskirts of Samaria, our beautiful capital city.

There beneath the oak tree is Gomer, my wife; I love her as I love my own life. You will learn to love her too. Sitting beside her is our son Jezreel. He is eighteen now, handsome and strong - a young man with a heart for God. At Gomer's feet and looking up at her is Ruhamah, our daughter. Do you see how her raven hair glistens. She is the image of her mother. She was seventeen just half a year ago. Beside her is Ammi, her brother. He is fifteen and as warm and bubbling as the flowing brook that you hear in the background.

We are happy and at peace. It has not always been so.

I began my ministry as a prophet almost thirty years ago during the reign of Jeroboam II. Those were years of prosperity in Israel. The caravans that passed between Assyria and Egypt paid taxes into the treasury of Jeroboam II and sold their goods in our midst. But they also left their sons and daughters and their gods. These gods of the Assyrians, the Egyptians, of the ancient Canaanites and of Jezebel have wooed the hearts of my people. Altars built for sin offerings have become places for sinning.

If you were to walk through my land today, you would see images and altars in all the green groves. My people have many sheep and cattle. Some think that Baal, the so-called fertility god, is the giver of lambs, of calves and the fruit of the field. Every city has its high place for the worship of Baal. There is a high place not far from here. At night we hear the beat of the priest's music and the laughter of the sacred prostitutes. Just last week a man and woman who live three houses from us placed their infant son as a human sacrifice in the flaming hands of the god Baal.

You may ask how Jehovah's people could sink to such unholy ways. It is because the priests of God have departed from Him. They delight in the sins of the people; they lap it up and lick their lips for more. Thus it is, "Like priests, like people." Because the priests are wicked, the people are wicked as well. God will surely judge. My beautiful land is just a few short years from being crushed under the iron heel of the Assyrian military might.

But you did not come to hear a story of gloom and sin but love and hope.

Yes, 30 years ago, God appointed me a prophet in Israel. My father, Beeri, and my honored mother taught me early to fear Jehovah, the one true God of Israel. They taught me to hate the calf deity of the first Jeroboam. Daily we prayed. Daily we longed to return to the Temple in Jerusalem. Daily we sang the songs of David and hungered for the coming of Messiah.

My ministry has always been hard. The first ten years were the hot-blooded days of my twenties. My sermons were sermons of fire. My heart bled for my people. I was little heeded and generally scorned. In my thirty-second year God stirred me and I spent many days in prayer and meditation. I felt lonely and in need of a companion.

The first frosts of fall had tinted the leaves when I traveled with my parents to visit the home of Diblaim. In the busy activity of ministry, I had not seen the family for several years. We were engaged in lively conversation when through the door swept a young woman, Gomer, the daughter of Diblaim. I remembered her as a pretty and somewhat spoiled child. Now she was a hauntingly beautiful woman. Her ivory face was framed in a wealth of raven black hair. Her striking beauty distracted me, and I had great difficulty in turning my eyes from her.

As we returned to our home that day, my father and I talked of many things. In my mind lingered the image of a raven-haired Israelite. My father's friendship with Diblaim flourished and often I journeyed with him to visit. I was drawn to Gomer. Diblaim and my father talked incessantly. Then one day my father astounded me with the proposal, "Hosea, it is my desire that you should marry Gomer."

I did not question that I loved Gomer. But something about her troubled me. As most young women of our time, she had a love for expensive clothing, jewelry and cosmetics. That I accepted as part of her womanhood. But she seemed experienced beyond her years in the ways of the world.

Yet, I loved her. It was my father's will that I should marry her. I knew that my burning love for Jehovah would win her from any wanton ways. God confirmed to me that indeed Gomer was His choice as well.

I wooed her with the passion of a prophet. God had given me the gift of poetry and I flooded Gomer with words of love.

She responded to my love. We stood together beneath the flower-strewn canopy of the Hebrew marriage altar, and pledged eternal love to God and to each other. We listened together to the reading of God's laws of marriage. We heard the reminder that our marriage was a symbol of the marriage between Jehovah and Israel, His wife.

I took Gomer to my home. We read together the Song of Songs which is Solomon's. We ate the sweet fruit of its garden of love. She was as refreshing to me as the first fig of the season. Gomer seemed content in the love of God and of Hosea. I looked forward to the future with hope.

Shortly after the anniversary of our 1st year of marriage, Gomer presented me with a son. I sought God's face and learned that his name was to be Jezreel - a name that would constantly remind Israel that God's judgment was surely coming. It was a stark reminder to me of the times in which we lived.

After the birth of Jezreel, Gomer changed. She became distant, and a sensual look flashed in her eye. I thought it a reaction to the responsibility of caring for our son. Those were busy days. The message of God inflamed me and I cried out across the land.

Gomer was soon with child again. This time a daughter was born. I learned from God that her name was to be Lo-Ruhamah. It was a strange name and troubled me deeply for it meant, "Not loved." For God said, "I will no longer show my love to the nation of Israel, that I should forgive her."

Gomer began to drift from me after that. Often she would leave after putting the children to bed and not return until dawn. She grew worn, haggard, and rebellious. I sought every way possible to restore her to me, but to no avail. About eighteen months later a third child was born, a boy. God told me to call him Lo-Ammi - meaning, "not my people."

God said to Israel, "You are not my people and I am not your God." In my heart a thorn was driven. I knew that Lo-Ammi was not my son and that his sister was not the fruit of my love. Those were days of deep despair. I could not sing the songs of David. My heart broke within me.

After Lo-Ammi was weaned, Gomer went beyond my reach and did not return. I became both father and mother to the three children.

I felt blight upon my soul. My ministry seemed paralyzed by the waywardness of my wife. My prayers seemed to sink downward. Then the Lord stirred me. I came to know that God was going to use my experience as an illustration of His love for Israel.

Love flamed again for Gomer and I knew that I could not give her up. I sought her throughout Samaria. I found her in the ramshackle house of a lustful, dissolute Israelite who lacked the means to support her. I begged her to return. She spurned all my pleadings.

Heavy-hearted I returned to the children, mourned, and prayed. My mind was warmed with a plan. I went to the market, bought food and clothing for Gomer. I bought the jewelry and the cosmetics she loved so dearly.

Then I sought out her lover in private. He was suspicious, thinking that I had come to do him harm. When I told him my plan, a sly smile crept over his face. He understood that if I could not take Gomer home, my love would not allow me to see her destitute. I would provide all her needs and she could think that they came from him.

We struck hands on the bargain. He struggled home under his load of provisions. I followed in the shadows.

Gomer met him with joy and showered him with love. She told him to wait outside the house while she replaced her dirty, worn apparel with the new. After what seemed hours, she reappeared, dressed in radiant splendor. Her lover approached to embrace her, but she held him off. I heard her say, "No, the clothes and food and cosmetics are not from your hand for where would you get them? Surely they are from the hand of Baal who gives all such things. I am resolved to express my gratitude to Baal by serving as a priestess at the high place."

I saw her walk away. She seemed like the rebellious heifer I had seen as a youth in my father's herd. She could not be helped but would go astray. The more I tried to restore her the further she went from me. Feeble with inner pain, I stumbled home to sleepless nights and days of confusion and grief.

Gomer gave herself with reckless abandonment to her role of priestess of Baal. She eagerly prostituted her body to the wanton will of the worshipers of the sordid deity.

My ministry became a pilgrimage of pain. I became an object of derision. It seemed that the penalty for the sin of Gomer and of all my people had settled upon me.

I fell back upon Jehovah. My father and mother aided me in the care and instruction of the three children. They responded in love and obedience. They became the Balm of Gilead for my wounded heart. The years passed as I sounded the burden of God throughout the land.

Daily I prayed for Gomer, and as I prayed, love for her sang in my soul. She was my nightly dream. A dream so real that on waking I often felt as if she had just left me again. The years flowed on but the priests of Baal held her in their deadly clutch.

It was just over a year ago that it happened. The blush of spring was beginning to touch our land. In the midst of my morning hour of meditation, God seemed to move me to go among the people of Samaria. A sense of deep anticipation stirred me. I wandered through the streets.

Soon I was standing in the slave market. It was a place I loathed. Then I saw a priest of Baal lead a woman to the slave block. My heart stood still. It was Gomer. A terrible sight she was to be sure, but it was Gomer. Stark naked she stood on the block. But no man stared in lust. She was broken, haggard, and thin as a wisp of smoke. Her ribs stood out beneath the skin. Her hair was matted and touched with streaks of gray, and in her eye was the flash of madness. I wept.

Then softly the voice of God's love whispered to my heart. I paused, confused. The bidding reached thirteen shekels of silver before I fully understood God's purposes. I bid fifteen shekels of silver. There was a pause. A voice on the edge of the crowd shouted "fifteen shekels and a homer of barley."

"Fifteen shekels, a homer and a half of barley," I cried. The bidding was done.

As I approached the slave block, a murmur of disbelief surged through the crowd. They knew me and they knew Gomer. As I mounted the block they leaned forward in anticipation. Surely I would strike her dead on the spot for her waywardness. But my heart flowed with love.

I stood in front of Gomer and cried out to the people. "God says, 'Unless Israel remove her adulteries from her, I will strip her as naked as the day she was born. I will make her as a desert place and leave her like a parched land to die of thirst'"

I spoke to a merchant at a nearby booth, "Bring that white robe on the end of the rack."

I paid him the price he asked. Then I drew the robe around Gomer's emaciated body and said to her, "Gomer, you are mine by the natural right of a husband. Now you are also mine because I have bought you for a price. You will no longer wander from me or play the harlot. You must be confined for a time and then I will restore you to the full joys of womanhood."

She sighed, and fainting fell into my arms. I held her and spoke to my people, "Israel will remain many days without king or prince, without sacrifice or ephod. Afterward Israel will return and seek the Lord her God and David her king. She will come trembling to the Lord and to His benefits in the last days. And where it was said of Israel, 'Lo-Ruhamah, you are not loved, it will be said Ruhamah, you are loved.' For the love of God will not give you up, but pursue you down your days. And where Israel was called, 'Lo-Ammi, you are not my people,' it will be said, 'Ammi, you are the people of the living God,' for I will forgive you and restore you."

I returned home with my frail burden. I nursed Gomer back to health. Daily I read to her the writings of God. I taught her to sing the penitential songs of David, and then together we sang the songs of David's joyful praise to God. In the midst of song I restored her to God, to our home, to our children.

Do you not see how beautiful she is? I have loved her always, even in the depth of her waywardness because my God loved her. Gomer responded to God's love and to mine. She does not call me "My master" but "my husband." And the name of Baal has never again been on her lips.

Now my people listen to my message with new responsiveness for I am a prophet that has been thrilled with a great truth. I have come to know in the depth of my being how desperately God loves sinners. How deliberately He seeks them! How devotedly He woos them to Himself!

*** Marriage Wisdom ***

Love each other unconditionally, with a sacrificial love, always ready to forgive and restore.

Hosea and Gomer
by Jean Garner

Hosea was a prophet, on fire for the Lord;
So burdened for his people, but they heeded not his word!
Israel, so idolatrous, in the lowest dregs of sin,
Worshipped heathen idols, and sacrificed to them.
Hosea's heart was broken, as was the Lord's also,
To think beloved Israel, could ever sink so low!
Then God sent Hosea, to choose himself a wife
From a family of whoredoms, whose lives with sin were rife;
And so he married Gomer – loved her despite her sin,
As a lesson to wayward Israel, the Lord was using him!
Gomer had three children – the Lord gave each a name,
Whose meaning pointed further to Israel's sin and shame.
This "Object Lesson Marriage" God was going to use
As a picture of the Lord, Himself, and the wicked, wayward Jews!

Hosea loved his little bride – would have filled her every need;
But Gomer left this haven, an adulterous life to lead.
He pleaded and he begged her to return and be his wife,
But she ignored his pleadings – she preferred her sinful life.
Just so Israel left their God and turned to worship Baal,
And Hosea's pleas for their return, were all to no avail!

Gomer sunk so very low and chose this life to lead,
But Hosea, without her knowing, still supplied her need.
Soon she lost her beauty; was thin, sad and depraved.
Then they placed her on the block to be sold a common slave!
God then told Hosea, to take his wife again,
Just as God loved Israel, though they caused Him so great pain!
She'd sunk so low, she was but worth half the price of a slave!
But Hosea tenderly carried her home, and tried her life to save.
Twas then she realized his love; confessed her sin and shame!
Surrounded by his love and care, she'd never stray again!

And so this pictures Israel, and God who loves them so;
Though He allows much punishment, He'll never let them go;
And will come a future day – much happiness to bring
When God, in person of His Son – on earth, will be their King!

JOSEPH & MARY
"Profound Love"

"For God so loved the world that He gave His only Son, that whosoever believes in Him will not perish, but have everlasting life."
John 3:16

Mary and Joseph were engaged to be married and like all engaged couples from the beginning of time, looked forward to the consummation of their marriage.

Neither one of these young people knew it, but something was about to happen that would change their direction. They were each going to be visited by an angel who would give them a message that would change their lives completely.

The Bride – Luke 1:26-38

What does Luke 1:26-27 tell us about Mary?
_____
_____

Who was the angel God sent, and what did he say to Mary? Luke 1:26-28_____
_____
_____

How did Mary respond to the angel? Luke 1:29
_____
_____

What did the angel say to Mary to comfort her? Luke 1:30
_____
_____

What message did the angel bring from God? Luke 1:31-33

_____
_____
_____
_____
_____

What question did Mary have? Luke 1:34 _____
_____

What was the remarkable answer to this question? Luke 1:35_____
_____
_____
_____

What additional information did the angel give her in Luke 1:36?_____
_____
_____

Wow! Here was a young teenage girl leading a normal life, getting ready for her marriage, when all of a sudden she's hit with this incredible proclamation from God. She must have thought, "This is impossible."

What does Luke 1:37 tell us?

_____

Mary had a choice to make when she knew God's plan for her. What was her decision? Luke 1:38

_____
_____

What further confirmation did she receive when she went to visit Elizabeth? Luke 1:39-42_____
_____
_____

What was the first part of Mary's song written in Luke 1:46-49 that showed her thankfulness for God's work in her life?

_____
_____
_____
_____
_____

The Groom – Matthew 1:18-25

What was the situation in Matthew 1:18?_____
_____

Joseph now had a dilemma - the child was not his; he and Mary had not had a physical relationship! What should he do?

Read Matthew 1:19 and write down the thoughts going through Joseph's mind:_____
_____
_____

What does this tell you about his character, and his love for Mary?_____
_____

The reason Joseph did not want to accuse Mary openly was because under the Law, Mary could be put to death for adultery. While Joseph was still wrestling with his dilemma, who appeared to him in a dream and what did he say? Matthew 1:20-21_____
_____
_____
_____
_____

In Matthew 1:22-23 the angel told Joseph that this baby would be the fulfillment of the prophecy in Isaiah 7:14)

Joseph now had to make a choice. What did he decide? Matthew 1:24-25 _____
_____
_____

Now turn to Luke 2:7 to witness the birth of their baby. What does it tell us? _____
_____
_____
_____

The angel of the Lord appeared once again, this time to shepherds out in the field. Summarize the announcement. Luke 2:10-12 _____
_____
_____
_____

Looking upward to God

*** *God is Eternal* ***

He is everlasting; without beginning or end. His plans were made before the foundation of the world.

John 1:1-2 _____
_____
_____

John 8:58 _____
_____
_____

From My Heart to Yours . . .

During the Christmas season we have shopping to do, presents to wrap, goodies to bake and cards to send. It is a hectic time for most people, yet God would like us to set aside time in the midst of our busyness to think about what Christmas really means.

The love story of Mary and Joseph is an awesome one. It is the story of two people who were willing to do the will of God no matter what the cost and no matter what others would think.

At the beginning of their relationship, they had to individually and decisively make the choice to do God's will; then together, they lived their lives in obedience to what the Heavenly Father revealed to them.

Mary is highly exalted in some religions to the point of being a god herself. Yet she was a sinner just like each one of us, born to earthly parents. "For all have sinned and come short of the glory of God." (Romans 3:23) Even Mary!

Mary was not perfect, but she was willing to be used of God, just as God still uses people today to accomplish His will. What a glorious thought - that as we yield ourselves to God, He will make something beautiful of our lives and bring glory to Himself.

I believe there are five reasons why God chose Mary for the "special" assignment of bringing the Savior into the world.

- ♥ Because of her pure character. Luke 1:27
  She was a virgin. Today virginity is mocked, yet God holds up moral purity as a standard from which we cannot escape if we want to please Him. Mary was a morally pure young lady.

- ♥ Because of her humility. Luke 1:48-49
  She didn't go around bragging that God had chosen her because she was so wonderful and better than others. She gave all glory to God for His grace and mercy in her life, and referred to herself as His servant.

- ♥ Because of her submissiveness to the will of God. Luke 1:35-38
  She obeyed because it was God directing her. Even if she didn't fully understand His will; even when it didn't seem possible, she stepped out in faith and accepted God's perfect will for her life. God uses willing vessels.

- ♥ Because of her love for God and His Word. Luke 1:46-55
  She knew who God was and the things He had done. She loved and worshipped Him, and made Him her focus.

- ♥ Because she was marrying a man who was of the royal seed of David. Luke 3:33-38; John 7:42
  It was prophesied that Jesus would come through the royal seed of David.

Mary and Joseph each had to make individual decisions and then as a couple.

Mary had to consider whether or not she wanted her nice, quiet, orderly life disrupted by giving herself completely to God? What would Joseph say? What would her parents and friends say? Would they believe she could still be a virgin and be pregnant? Would they believe it was a Holy God and not a lustful man who did this to her? Would they believe that the promised Messiah would come through her . . . their Mary? She could hardly believe it herself.

Joseph's decision had to take into consideration the fact that life was no longer uncomplicated and carefree. Did he want to take on the responsibility of being married to a woman who would be the mother of the Son of God? Was he spiritually capable of handling this?

In the end, they each made an individual decision to obey God no matter what and they proved their love for God by putting Him first, instead of themselves.

And because of their individual commitment to the Lord, they were strong in their "couple commitment" also, and the promised Messiah was born.

This was the beginning of many joys and many sorrows for this young couple with their special son, but God was truly with them through it all.

And again, although Mary and Joseph were a privileged couple, and God had given them the very important job of bringing up His Son, they are not to be highly exalted or worshipped in any way.

The child born to them would also be their Savior. They were both sinners and needed the Savior to make an atonement for their sin so that they could spend eternity with Him in Heaven.

When Jesus came, it was the beginning of a White Christmas for everyone - "Come now, and let us reason together saith the Lord; though your sins be as scarlet, they shall be as white as snow." (Isaiah 1:18)

Think about what this special child born to Mary and Joseph means in your life today? (John 3:16) Has it changed your life?

> *** *Marriage Wisdom* ***
>
> Obey God individually, and as a couple, and God will bless you and use you greatly for His glory

Joseph and Mary
by Jean Garner

A very special couple: They were highly in God's favor
Chosen as the earthly parents of our Lord and Savior!
When Gabriel appeared one day with the message from the Lord,
Mary said: "I am His child! Be it according to His Word!"
And so the mighty Son of God chose to come to earth
By way of this sweet virgin's womb, and by a lowly birth.

Poor Joseph was beside himself! He'd thought Mary to be true!
His betrothed is now with child, whatever will he do!
He decided he'd protect her; he'd surround her with his love,
It was then his answer came – instructions from above!
"Fear not to take your Mary, and keep her in your care,
For 'tis the Son of God Himself – the babe that she will bear!"

And when the time was drawing near that Jesus would be born,
All were ordered to be taxed back in their own home town.
So Joseph went with Mary to the town from which he came;
Even back to David's city – Bethlehem by name.
Crowds of people pushed their way! The tall, the fat, the thin!
When Joseph came with Mary, there was no room in the Inn!
There was a stable right near by hewn from out the rock;
It had lots of hay and straw to feed the owner's stock.
Little Mary, tired and worn, was thankful for the hay.
Ere morning broke, the babe was born and in the manger lay.

The shepherds on the hillside were watching o'er their flock,
When suddenly the sky lit up and they got quite a shock!
First there was one angel, and then a host of them,
Saying: "Glory to God in the highest; peace, good will to men!
For unto you is born this day, in Bethlehem, a babe,
None other than the Son of God – within a manger laid.
So they hurried to the place they'd heard the angels say,
And worshipped there, the tiny babe, on that first Christmas day.

AQUILA & PRISCILLA
"Compatible Love"

*"Oh, magnify the Lord with me
and let us exalt His name together."*
Psalm 34:3

The prophet Amos asks a probing question in Amos 3:3. What is it? _____
_____

Young couples contemplating marriage would be wise to think deeply upon that question and determine in their hearts what they can do to have unity in their marriage.

Priscilla and Aquila were a blessing to the Apostle Paul, and he counted them among his best friends. Where were Aquila and Priscilla from, how did Paul get together with them, and what did they have in common? Acts 18:1-3

_____
_____
_____
_____

What did Paul do while in Corinth, besides tent-making, and what were the results of his work? Acts 18:4-5 _____
_____
_____
_____

When the Jews fought among themselves regarding Jesus, Paul decided to go to the gentiles with his message. What was the result of that? Acts 18:7-8 _____
_____
_____

How long did Paul stay in Corinth and what was his main objective? Acts 18:11 _____
_____

As Aquila and Priscilla worked alongside Paul in their home and listened to his preaching, he was making disciples of them. When he left for Ephesus, Paul took this couple with him and left them there to start a church.

Paul, while training Aquila and Priscilla for leadership, was doing what he told Timothy to do in II Timothy 2:2. What does that verse tell us? _____
_____
_____

In this way, many more people could be reached with the gospel than Paul trying to do it all by himself. Paul was able to leave Aquila and Priscilla to work in the church at Ephesus while he went elsewhere to preach.

It was there in Ephesus that Aquila and Priscilla met a Jewish preacher named Apollos whom they discipled much in the same way Paul discipled them.

Describe Apollos and his preaching. Acts 18:24-25
_____
_____
_____
_____
_____
_____

When they heard Apollos preach boldly in the synagogue, what did Aquila and Priscilla do? Acts 18:26
_____
_____

The KJV version of the Bible says that they "expounded." What is the dictionary meaning of expound? _____
_____
_____

They didn't just tell him that Messiah had come, they proved it by the Scriptures. In order to teach Apollos, they needed God's wisdom. How is this wisdom described in James 3:17? _____
_____
_____

The following verses hint at the prominence Aquila and Priscilla in the early church, and what they meant to Paul:

Romans 16:3-5a _____
_____
_____
_____
_____

I Corinthians 16:19 _____
_____
_____

Paul's great esteem for this couple is shown in what is believed to be his last letter when he tells Timothy to greet Priscilla and Aquila (II Timothy 4:19).

Unity among believers, and especially between married partners, is something we all need to strive for. Write out the following verses:

Romans 14:19 _____
_____
_____

Romans 15:6 _____
_____
_____

II Corinthians 13:11 _____
_____
_____

Ephesians 4:3 _____
_____

Building "oneness" in marriage takes humility, love and planning. You need to have "couple" goals, and also help each other in individual goals as well. The more you can enjoy doing together, the closer you become. You are a team, not opponents. This takes perseverance and practice.

List some ways you can draw closer to your mate in the following areas. Be creative:

Work/Chores	**Faith**
Learning	**Ministry**

Children	**Finances**
Recreation	**Romance**

Looking upward to God

> ### **** God is Omniscient ****
>
> He knows everything. He knows the end from the beginning. He has all the answers and will freely give wisdom and understanding to His children when they ask.
>
> Jeremiah 17:10 _____
> _____
> _____
> _____
>
> James 1:5 _____
> _____
> _____
> _____

From My Heart to Yours . . .

We often hear the saying that "opposites attract" and that may very well be true. However, there is also much to be said for a couple who are much alike in their attitudes, talents and goals.

Two people going in the same direction in life will arrive at their destination in better shape than two people who are pulling in different directions. And they will have the joy of uninterrupted fellowship and unity along the way.

Aquila and Priscilla had a unity of spirit that few couples ever achieve, but most envy. Even their names rhyme, for heaven's sake! We don't find any striving in this marriage, just a simple working together in all aspects of their lives, to bring glory to God.

They must have been a shining example to their neighbors of what God intended marriage to be, and I'm sure many came to know Christ as Savior through visiting their home.

The Bible has a lot to say about being a light in the midst of darkness.

> "Let your light so shine before men, that they may see your good works, and glorify your Father, who is in heaven."
> Matthew 5:16

> "For ye were once darkness, but now you are light in the Lord; walk as children of light."
> Ephesians 5:8

> "That you may be blameless and harmless, children of God, without rebuke, in the midst of a crooked and perverse nation, among whom you shine as lights in the world."
> Philippians 2:15

The world desperately needs Christian couples and Christian families who will be "lights" in their neighborhoods, leading people to the Light of the world, Jesus Christ.

We don't have to be as compatible as Priscilla and Aquila, but we do need to have unity as our goal. And in order to do that we need to focus on what God wants for our marriage, and then make goals, and aim for those goals. We need to serve God and we need to learn to serve one another.

My husband and I started out as complete opposites and there was a lot of arguing and fighting and selfishness and walking in different directions. When we came to know the Lord, we knew we had to do things differently, and little by little over the years we have made great progress and have had a happy and satisfying marriage.

We started off by putting God first and went to Bible school together. During that time we also enjoyed an exciting trip to Israel that we will always remember.

I knew I couldn't continue to be selfish - I had to focus on my husband's needs and not just my own.

I couldn't continue to think that during a disagreement he was always wrong and I was always right (Whatttt?). I'm still struggling with that one. ☺ And, of course, I had to give up on the idea that he could read my mind.

Even though some of our interests are very different, I had to learn to stop ignoring his and take an interest in what he was doing and let him talk about it without my eyes glazing over.

Now we share chores around the house. He mainly takes care of the outside and keeps up the flower and vegetable gardens we have all year round in FL. I encourage him and enjoy the beauty of our yard and all the delicious veggies I get to eat. We're also able to share with the neighbors and we freeze vegetables for year round enjoyment.

We both like to cook and decided we would each choose a night each week to make something brand new that we never tried before as a surprise for each other. So for at least two nights each week, we have the excitement of trying some new culinary treats. If they turn out badly, we can turn it into a date night and go out for pizza or tacos. But so far what we've made is delicious. My husband came up with a wonderful recipe for spaghetti pizza, with the crust being the spaghetti. It was so good and he is happy when he sees me taking an extra helping.

I mainly take care of the inside of the house, cleaning, decorating, painting, laundry, organizing. I love this. All except for vacuuming . . .

When I had surgery many years ago, my doctor told me not to vacuum. So my husband volunteered to do the vacuuming, and 25 years later he is still doing it. Haha. I don't have inclination to tell him it was only supposed to be for a few months. Hey, this is a good deal! Shhhhhh.

We do like the same TV shows, and what little television we watch, we watch together and often hold hands. Both of us like snacks at night and look forward to those.

We both teach life groups at church, and even though we teach different ones, we take an interest in what the other one is teaching and what's happening with the class and help each other out as much as possible. We sit in church together and enjoy the music, message and fellowship.

One of the greatest things we do in recent years is pray together each day and discuss spiritual things. Saying "I love you" many times daily gives us a real sense of security and comfort, especially during the trials of life.

We have come to appreciate each other's differences and to see how we complement each other and balance each other out.

We have a kitty cat named Braveheart that we both love and we spend a lot of time playing with him and laughing. Sometimes we wake up in the middle of the night to find Braveheart stretched out full-length beside us with his head on the pillow! It makes us both laugh.

My husband recently took up bike riding and is planning to take part in a Senior Marathon in the near future. Although this type of activity doesn't interest me on a personal level, I can cheer him on and pray for him and make sure he has everything he needs as far as bike gear and clothing, etc.

We both belong to the YMCA, and although we haven't been in a while, when we do go, I usually head off to Zumba class and he heads in to use the exercise equipment. We plan to start using the pool together.

I love to do counted cross-stitch, and my husband is always there complimenting my work and cheering me on as I make projects to give to relatives and friends.

Another thing we do is to plan special events for each other's birthdays, our anniversary and vacations, and get a great deal of enjoyment out of this. One year he kidnapped me and took me for a trip throughout New England, and one year I kidnapped him and took him to CA to see our daughter. Fun times of building good memories.

For the last few years, we've both been doing a lot of writing and reminiscing as we worked on our life stories and had them published as a legacy for our children and grandchildren. I also wrote a Welch family cookbook with favorite recipes and memories, and my hubby wrote a book from the viewpoint of Braveheart our cat. We published both of those as well.

I have been working on four women's Bible studies for publication, one of which you hold in your hands.

And my hubby has been working on a DVD series, student notes and a book for Grief Care Fellowship to train grief mentors to come alongside people who are grieving the death of a loved one. We go over each other's material and try to offer helpful suggestions and encouragement which sparks greater creativity in both of us.

We love to take our grandkids out to eat when they have the time and we love having everyone here for Christmas. This is a good time of life for us and we're enjoying it. We have made plenty of mistakes along the way, but with God's help we have persevered, learned from them, used them to help others, and seek to finish well.

Nothing in our lives happened by accident - we had to purpose to make it happen. Remember that in marriage, just like anything else, all things are possible with God. Love and serve each other, and keep your eyes on the finish line where Jesus waits and smiles.

We are definitely not Aquila and Priscilla, but we do have unity and love

---

*** *Marriage Wisdom* ***

Be of one mind towards God, each other, and your ministry, and you will be a light in the darkness of the world.

Aquila and Priscilla
by Jean Garner

God instituted marriage, way back when time began.
A happy family unit was a part of God's great plan!
And so man leaves his father's house and searches out a mate;
But God must do the choosing if to her he would relate!
They must work and walk together even though the way is hard,
If they would have a happy marriage and their lives count for the Lord!

Aquila and Priscilla seemed to have just such a life.
We hear of no divisions between this husband and his wife.
They had a unity of spirit few couples e'er achieve,
And their shining Christian spirit led others to believe.
They were a Jewish couple who lived and worked in Rome,
When through Claudius, the ruler, they were forced to leave their home!
And so they moved to Corinth and met the Apostle Paul,
Who was there to preach the Word of God and give his Gospel call!
They invited Paul to live with them – tent making was their trade,
And since it was Paul's work as well, he gladly with them stayed.
And so they worked together and listened as Paul preached.
They became proficient, so that others they could teach!
When Paul left for Ephesus, these two went with him there;
Here, a church, begun by Paul, was given to their care.

We never hear a mention of just one of them alone;
Always "Aquila and Priscilla" – the two seemed to be as one,
And so they worked ,in harmony in the ministry with Paul;
When he left for Syria, they were ready at his call!
They three came to Ephesus, and met Apollos there;
A man who knew the Scripture, and for preaching had a flair!
But he knew just the old-time scriptures; preached baptism, but of John!
Aquila nd Priscilla knew his theology was wrong;
So they took aside Apollos, and explained it word for word;
The Gospel of the Savior as from Apostle Paul they'd heard.
Apollos shoed how great a man and Christian that he proved
By listening to their discourse, and preaching as he should!
So every time they're mentioned; these two are highly praised,
A devoted, loving couple – served God through all their days!

Marriage Scrambles

Unscramble the letters to discover the names of married people of the Bible we have studied.

_____	AQUAIL
_____	MADA
_____	MEGRO
_____	HOPPARIT
_____	AHON
_____	VEE
_____	BANAL
_____	SHJOPE
_____	SHABBEHAT
_____	HABMARA
_____	IVADD
_____	RAMY
_____	ASHOE
_____	OBJ
_____	KEERBAH
_____	LAPISCRIL
_____	ASHAR
_____	CAISA
_____	BIGALIA

"For Better or For Worse"

Name the married couples

Our first baby son died but our second son was a royally smart guy!

We travelled a lot and started our very own nation.

We moved from Italy to Corinth and made tents with Paul.

We had a perfect marriage, but we blew it for ourselves and everyone.

We had three children with funny names, and after a short separation, reunited at an auction block

We are "Beauty and the Beast" – a nasty selfish beast and a wise and kind beauty who pacified a future king.

We clung together through stormy times even though the whole world was against us.

We met in a field for the first time and immediately consummated our marriage. Later we had twins.

We managed to stick together through better and worse. The better was blissful, but the worse was worse than boils.

Our first child did not match the DNA of one of us, but God had a special plan for our baby that would touch people's lives down through the ages.

We lived in Egypt and were quite well off until a handsome foreign slave became a real temptation to one of us. We had the slave thrown into prison.

www.ingramcontent.com/pod-product-compliance
Lightning Source LLC
Chambersburg PA
CBHW022305060426
42446CB00007BA/590